PORTRAIT OF
KARL BARTH

PORTRAIT OF

Translated, with an Introduction

by

ROBERT McAFEE BROWN

GEORGES CASALIS

KARL BARTH

GREENWOOD PRESS, PUBLISHERS
WESTPORT, CONNECTICUT

Library of Congress Cataloging in Publication Data

Casalis, Georges.
    Portrait of Karl Barth.

    Reprint of the 1st ed. published by Doubleday,
Garden City, N.Y.
        Bibliography: p.
        1. Barth, Karl, 1886–1968. I. Title.
[BX4827.B3C313 1981]   230'.44'0924   80-25829
ISBN 0-313-22775-6 (lib. bdg.)

This little book is dedicated to the "Theological Study Group" of the parish of St. Nicholas in Strasbourg, at whose eager and repeated insistence I prepared this guidebook, and who had come to know Karl Barth so well before they spent the unforgettable evening with him on November 22, 1959.

Georges Casalis

Kapf ob Eggiwil in Emmental
Easter 1959

This is a reprint of the first U.S. edition.

Published by arrangement with Doubleday & Company, Inc.

Reprinted in 1981 by Greenwood Press
A division of Congressional Information Service, Inc.
88 Post Road West, Westport, Connecticut 06881

Printed in the United States of America

10 9 8 7 6 5 4 3 2 1

PREFACE

After he had read the manuscript of this "portrait" and had corrected some minor inaccuracies, Karl Barth wrote the following brief note to the author:

"Concerning the work as a whole I have only one reservation which I shall not put in my own words, but in the words of a text which I happened to read recently.

"After the election of the new Pope, the Cardinal Archbishop of Toledo and Primate of Spain issued a pastoral letter to which the Pope responded as follows:

" 'Most beloved Eminence: Thank you more than I can say for your pastoral letter about the new Pope. May the Lord forgive you for the overabundant praises that you have bestowed on my humble person, and may he help me to bear fruit on the way to sanctity. Ever from my heart I greet you and bless you in all affection.

" 'John XXIII, Pope.'[1]

"You will understand that I feel a certain embarrassment when confronted by a book so full of praise of myself. But if I close my ears to the 'overabundant praises,' I can assert here

[1] *Herder-Korrespondenz*, XIII, 7, p. 322.

that you have understood my thought very well indeed, and that in your survey I have discovered to my joy the same intent which is at the foundation of my own life and work.

Sincerely,

KARL BARTH"

CONTENTS

Preface   v

Introduction, by Robert McAfee Brown   1

PART I   *Introduction*   34

PART II   *The Direction of Barth's Life*   38

Theological studies   40
The Epistle to the Romans   43
The *Dogmatics*   48
1933!   50
Theologische Existenz heute   53
Barmen   55
Continued witness to the faith   57
The letters to the churches   59
Spokesman for the defeated Germans   60
Barth and communism   68
The atomic bomb   73
Christians and public life   75
The Humanity of God   77
Mozart   80
The "big book"   81

PART III A *Critical Analysis of Barth's Principal Works*   83

I. Exegetical works   83
   Commentaries   83
   Books of sermons   88
II. Historical works   94
III. Dogmatic works   99
   The shorter works   100
   The *Church Dogmatics*   104
IV. Political and literary works   117
   Political works   117
   Literary works   120
V. The echo   122

PART IV *Conclusion*   124

A note on dialectical method   127
Bibliography of English writings   132
Translator's note   136

INTRODUCTION

by

Robert McAfee Brown

Theology . . . is a peculiarly beautiful science. Indeed, we can confidently say that it is the most beautiful of all the sciences. To find the sciences distasteful is the mark of the Philistine. It is an extreme form of Philistinism to find, or to be able to find, theology distasteful. The theologian who has no joy in his work is not a theologian at all. Sulky faces, morose thoughts and boring ways of speaking are intolerable in this science.

Karl Barth, *Church Dogmatics*, II/1, p. 656

A book about Karl Barth had better be very big or very small: very big because so much must be said to do justice to the subject matter, or very small because not everything can be said that should be said, and yet something must be said.

The present book, by deliberate intent, belongs in the latter category. It purports to be no more than its title suggests—a "portrait"—and the purpose of the present introduction is not to make a small book just a bit bigger, but to make the lines in the portrait clearer to those for whom it was not originally painted—English-speaking readers for whom the name of Karl Barth has always been something of a mystery.

Barth's recent visit to America—his first and only one in seventy-six active years—has dispelled some of the sense of mystery and theological austerity that surrounds the usual

American stereotype of a continental professor of theology, a professor who has written a six-million-word, seven-thousand-page, twelve-volume *Dogmatics*, still unfinished, not to mention forty or fifty other books and several hundred learned articles. The American public was as surprised as it was pleased that such a man should turn out to be a very human individual, possessing a shrewd sense of humor, incessantly smoking a large pipe and wearing a beret at a jaunty angle, more interested in visiting American prisons, the *avant-garde* theater and the Gettysburg battlefields than in making the conventional ecclesiastical sight-seeing tour.

So some of the American resistance to Barth himself has been neutralized by his much publicized visit, and it may be that this can serve as a prelude to the neutralization of much of the American resistance to his thought, a resistance heretofore based largely on a combination of ignorance and willingness to read Barth at second hand through the eyes of polemical interpreters.

I

This is not the opening gambit in a plea for Americans to become Barthians, and the point must be labored for a moment if anything that follows is to make sense. Whether one likes Barth's theology or not, he possesses major stature among Christian thinkers, and subsequent theology, whether following him or departing from him, can never again proceed without taking him into account. One can responsibly disagree with Barth; one cannot responsibly ignore him. Nor can one, any longer, assume that his own point of view need not reckon with the challenge that Barth's theology offers. Such an assumption will henceforth indicate only theological parochialism—or timidity.

But Americans parroting a Barthian line would only be parodying it. The most Barth can do is to force Americans to do what he himself has always done—to listen afresh to Scripture in the life of the church, not to reinforce a Barthian theology but to see how and in what ways the Word of God is speaking a fresh, challenging, upsetting and yet ultimately renewing word to the church and thereby to the world. "Barth's greatness," Paul Tillich writes, "is that he corrects himself again and again in the light of the 'situation,' and that he strenuously tries not to become his own follower."[1] And Barth, it is reliably reported, having seen the woodenness and theological *rigor mortis* that can infect the disciple of a human master, has been heard to mutter, "Thank God I am not a Barthian!"

Dogmatics is not written to call attention to the writer of dogmatics, but to call attention to the subject of dogmatics, namely Jesus Christ. People sometimes forget this, and Barth realizes that it will be the particular temptation of the dogmatician and his pupils to do so. And so he says,

> The angels laugh at old Karl. They laugh at him because he tries to grasp the truth about God in a book of Dogmatics. They laugh at the fact that volume follows volume and each is thicker than the previous one. As they laugh, they say to one another, "Look! Here he comes now with his little pushcart full of volumes of the *Dogmatics!*"
> And they laugh about the men who write so much about Karl Barth instead of writing about the things he is trying to write about. Truly, the angels laugh.[2]

This means, quite simply, that it would be a betrayal of everything for which Barth has worked, and fought, in the life of the church if a cult arose dedicated to the proposition that the *Church Dogmatics* should become a twentieth-century Protestant *Summa Theologica*. In one of the most illuminating single comments available on what Barth has attempted, Gabriel Vahanian has written, "A reformed theologian never

[1] Paul Tillich, *Systematic Theology*, I, University of Chicago Press, Chicago, 1951, p. 5.
[2] Quoted in an article by Johannes A. Lombard in *Antwort*, Evangelischer Verlag AG, Zollikon-Zürich, 1956, p. 895.

writes for posterity. He exhibits the living Word today."[3] And
Barth himself, whether he is dealing with the perfections of
God, or the doctrine of predestination, or the way a Christian
should deal with communism, has a disarming way of saying
in effect, "You don't like this way of dealing with the problem?
Well, then, propose another way and we will see if it is any
better."

What Barth has said about the relationship of contemporary theologians to the church fathers preceding them must
mutatis mutandis be applied to our relationship to him:

> There can be as little question of a repristination of the teaching
> of Luther and Calvin as of the orthodoxy of the 17th century, in
> the present rediscovery and reacknowledgement of the authority
> of the Reformers. If there were, we would not be giving them the
> honor due to them, but refusing it. Not those who repeat the
> doctrine most faithfully, but those who reflect upon it most faith-
> fully so that they can expound it as their own doctrine, are their
> most faithful pupils.[4]

The church of today must listen to the fathers, even though
it may disagree with the way the fathers stated things. The
church of today does the fathers a disservice if it merely
quotes them, trying to preserve unchanged their all-too-human
reactions to the gospel.

The Church of today would not be accepting them if it were
simply accepting or reproducing them in their historical form. It
would be accepting them not as the Church of today, not obedient
to its own calling along the lines of the Reformation, but as an
institute of antiquities—the worst dishonor of which it could be
guilty for all its well-meant veneration.[5]

[3] In the introduction to Barth, *The Faith of the Church*, Meridian Books,
New York, 1958, p. 9.
[4] Barth, *Church Dogmatics*, I/2, T. & T. Clark, Edinburgh, 1936, p. 619.
[5] *Ibid.*

This is why Barth can say, and apparently honestly mean it, that when he has finally finished the *Church Dogmatics*, it will be time for someone to begin the task all over again for the next generation. This does not mean that his work will go on the discard heap, or that dogmatics is really an expendable luxury in the life of the church, but that theology is an ongoing process, never completed, never perfect, always in need of restating in a new situation, and that he who tries to freeze the process, or halt it, is guilty of the worst sin possible, that of transforming a man-made product into something divine and unchangeable, and of reducing the life of the church to "an institute of antiquities." A Reformed theologian writes only for today.

II

If it can be taken for granted that it would be theologically improper as well as personally dishonoring to try to produce "Barthians," we can then examine more dispassionately, and without special pleading, some of the things Barth may have to say to the American theological scene, in the light of what we learn of him from M. Casalis' "portrait." The first step on this journey is to disabuse ourselves of some of the stereotypes Americans still have about Barth. At least four deserve comment:

1. Americans often accuse Barth of being pessimistic and quietistic. He is described as one of those gloomy continental theologians, so caught up in Pauline analyses of sin and judgment and crisis that all he can do is preach doom and catastrophe and human impotence. Since man can do nothing, all must be left to God. A parody of the activistic American hymn, "Rise Up, O Men of God," expresses the stereotype perfectly:

Sit down, O men of God,
His Kingdom He will bring,
Just as and when and where He will,
You cannot do a thing.

To be sure, Barth has written many words about sin, but he has also stressed the fact that we only know about sin because we already know about grace; it is only because we know that the power of sin has already been conquered by the power of God that we know how ominous is the adversary from whom we have already been delivered.[6] If Barth is someday adjudged a great heretic, it will not be for his pessimism, but for his optimism! He is without doubt the most hopeful of the contemporary theologians, so sure of the conquering power of the grace of God that he actually has a hard time finding a place for evil in his theology. The charge of theological pessimism is wide of the mark.

So too the charge of quietism. Whether or not one quite understands why Barth's theology has led him to such political activism, the fact of the matter is that it has. Some will argue that his political concerns derive elsewhere than from his mature theology, but that theology and ethics must go hand in hand is a built-in assumption of Barth's theology. M. Casalis' tracing of Barth's part in the German church struggle indicates the degree of his involvement, and Barth's writing during the war years show how impossible it was for him ever to theologize in a vacuum.[7]

2. Another American criticism of Barth has been the charge that he stresses the transcendence or otherness of God in a

[6] Cf. the structure of *Church Dogmatics*, Volume IV, where in each "part-volume" it is only in the light of a previous Christological affirmation that it is then possible to see the true dimensions of sin.
[7] Cf. Arthur C. Cochrane, *The Church's Confession Under Hitler*, Westminster Press, Philadelphia, 1962, for an account of the events up through Barmen (1934). Many of Barth's writings during these years have never been translated, but there are two collections in German of the most important documents: *Karl Barth zum Kirchenkampf* (*Theologische Existenz heute*, Heft 49), Chr. Kaiser Verlag, München, 1956, and *Eine Schweizer Stimme*, 1938–1945, Evangelischer Verlag AG, Zollikon-Zürich, 1945.

one-sided way. There is some historical justification for this feeling in light of the fact that for many years the only works of Barth available in English were his early writings, notably *The Epistle to the Romans,* where the famous statements occur that God is "Wholly Other," that if Barth has a system it is based on Kierkegaard's belief in the infinitely qualitative distinction between God and Man, and that as Ecclesiastes reminds us, God is in heaven and we are on earth.

However, as the volumes of Barth's *Dogmatics* show in great detail and as his little essay on *The Humanity of God* shows in brief compass, this emphasis was only a needed corrective at the moment, which has had its own corrective long since in Barth's writings. In the *Dogmatics,* particularly in Volume IV, it is emphasized that God is *not* just "in heaven"; he has taken the long, hard road of becoming man, engaged in what Barth has called "the journey of the Son of God into the far country." The *deity* of God is thus expressed precisely in the *humanity* of a God who is not "other" and aloof, but who has come incredibly near, so near as to endure nail prints in torn flesh.

3. Americans often accuse Barth of being theologically rigid, a ponderous orthodox thinker at the far right of the theological spectrum, reviving outdated thinkers like Calvin, Luther and the Protestant scholastics, not to mention medievalists like Anselm, and using the Bible in a way far too close to fundamentalism to make any save the fundamentalists happy.[8]

But no one who reads very far in the *Dogmatics,* or even in the smaller works, can rest content with the notion of Barth as representing orthodoxy *redivivus.* He is actually a rather daring innovator, as we shall try to illustrate later. If liberals find him too traditional to suit their fancy, they can

[8] Actually, the fundamentalists are among those most unhappy about Barth's use of the Bible, and they consider him a particularly dangerous heretic because much of the time he *sounds* orthodox enough to confuse people into thinking that he really is. Barth's treatment of Scripture is contained in *Church Dogmatics,* I/2, especially pp. 457–740.

rest assured that the conservatives do not find him to their liking. No orthodox Calvinist could accept Barth's treatment of election, for Barth decisively breaks with orthodox Calvinism's interpretation of double predestination. He rejects the traditional view of the plenary inspiration of Scripture, acknowledging the existence of errors in the text, and even glorying (from a theological point of view) in the fact that God speaks through the pages of a fallible text, so that the text will not be an end in itself, but a witness beyond itself to Jesus Christ, who, like the text, comes to us in full humanity. Rather than accusing Barth of resting too comfortably in the folds of orthodoxy, one ought rather to complain that he shakes orthodoxy up so much that it can never be the same again—if, indeed, that need be cause for complaint.

But Barth does none of this for the sake of novelty. He does it for the sake of the gospel. Commenting on the reformulating he had done in the *Dogmatics*, he wrote in 1949:

> In none of these fields could I simply go along with an accepted church doctrine and theological position; I had to think through and develop everything anew, from a center which I considered the right one—namely the Old and New Testament witness to the person and work of Jesus Christ.[9]

4. Another frequent American criticism of Barth has been the charge that he is anticultural. So much does he stress the uniqueness of Christian revelation, so vehemently does he reject natural theology and the insights of "religion," that he seems to isolate the Christian, placing him in a private world of his own where he can learn nothing save what he learns directly from God's Word. There is no path from culture to Christ, which would appear to suggest that there is no path from Christ to culture. The isolation of Christian thought from all other thought would seem to result.

But here again, misunderstanding seems to be responsible for such an estimate. It is true that Barth feels that the path

[9] In *The Christian Century*, March 16, 1949, p. 334.

from human knowledge to knowledge of God is a *cul de sac*, for reasons we shall presently examine. But this does not make conversation and understanding and mutual enrichment impossible between theology and culture; it simply means that conversation and understanding and mutual enrichment do not proceed solely on the premises of those who reject Christian revelation out of hand. In response to a query on this point by the present writer, Barth responded, "Look, I do not live in an ivory turret. I teach in a university and I talk with my colleagues. I have lunch with a philosopher and he tells me how it looks to him from his standpoint, and then I tell him how it looks to me in the light of Christian revelation. And then we see what happens. . . ."[10]

What Barth seems determined to preserve in his constant interplay with the cultural forces around him is the right of the Christian to make judgments from within the purview of his Christian faith, rather than having to bracket his faith and think, speak and act from an alien viewpoint. An excellent example of his procedure is furnished in III/2 of the *Dogmatics*, dealing with the doctrine of man. Barth examines the contemporary answers to the question "What is man?" that are given by scientific humanism, idealistic ethics and existentialism. Rejecting these as doing insufficient justice to their subject matter, Barth then answers the question "What is man?" by inviting his readers to look with him at one who was "true man," Jesus Christ. Only in him do we see man rightly and adequately defined for us. However, once he has firmly established this Christological basis for a doctrine of man, Barth reexamines what science, ethics and existentialism tell us about man, and finds much corroborative material in them that is useful to the Christian. Rather than rejecting culture, Barth attempts to appropriate creatively from it. And if one objects to the arbitrariness of his approach, it can be replied that this is no more arbitrary, methodologically, than

[10] On this matter, see further Barth's essay on "The Christian Message and the New Humanism," in *Against the Stream*, S. C. M. Press, London, 1954, pp. 181–191.

the way the scientist, the ethicist and the existentialist deal with similar material.

Similarly, Barth is sometimes charged with being antiphilosophical, or at least with being uninterested in philosophical questions. Greatly influenced by Kierkegaard in his early writings, one of the things Barth did in rewriting his *Dogmatics* was to purge it of Kierkegaardian influence:

> I have cut out of this second issue of the book [he wrote in 1933] everything that in the first issue might give the slightest appearance of giving to theology a basis, support, or even a mere justification in the way of existential philosophy.[11]

Barth was not dismissing Kierkegaard ungratefully, but making sure that his own theology was not molded (and consequently warped) by a single philosophical framework. Barth would be the last person in the world to assert that a theologian can operate independently of philosophical assumptions. He readily admits that when a human being starts to think or speak, he thinks or speaks philosophically. But the philosophy must serve the purposes of the gospel, rather than dictating the nature, or the substance, or the form of the gospel. If certain philosophical presuppositions distort that gospel, they must be jettisoned. Philosophy is a good servant but a bad master. It does not seem to matter too much to Barth which philosophical assumptions are employed, provided they are useful and provided they are subsidiary.[12]

So the American stereotypes of Barth as pessimistic and quietistic, believing only in divine transcendence, and exhibiting theological rigidity with a built-in anticultural bent, are all

[11] *Church Dogmatics*, I/1, Foreword, p. ix.
[12] The clearest treatment of this matter is in *Church Dogmatics*, I/2, pp. 727–736, 774–775. Barth's philosophical perception and his incorporation of philosophical critique is illustrated *inter alia* in *Church Dogmatics*, III/1, where he has long sections on Marcion and Schopenhauer (pp. 334–340), Descartes (pp. 350–363), and Leibniz (pp. 388–414), and in III/2, where he treats Fichte (pp. 96–109) and has extended comments on contemporary existentialism.

to be rejected. To whatever degree they might have possessed validity in connection with some of his early writings, that validity has been *passé* since at least 1936, when the first "part-volume" of the *Church Dogmatics* appeared in English. That the next "part-volume" did not appear in English until 1956—twenty years later—is cause for dismay, but no longer adequate cause for misunderstanding.

III

The difficulty many Americans feel with Barth's theology can be focused in an area where the issue is not misunderstanding, but a real difference of outlook. And there is one area where we can clearly join the issue between Barth and his American audience. This is found in Barth's vigorous and unyielding repudiation of what is usually known as "natural theology," the assumption (so built-in to the American temperament) that valid knowledge of God can be found apart from the revelation he has given of himself in Jesus Christ.[13]

The most clever *tour de force* of recent theological history was undoubtedly Barth's justification for accepting an invitation to give the Gifford Lectures on natural theology. In his opening lecture he pointed out that it would be to the benefit of believers in natural theology to learn what it is *not*, to be exposed to its complete antithesis, so that they could assess the position in which they disbelieved.

It can only be to the good of "Natural Theology" to be able once again to measure itself as the truth—if it is the truth!—by that which from its point of view is the greatest of errors. Opportunity is to be given it to do this here.[14]

[13] Barth's fullest treatment of this problem is found in *Church Dogmatics*, II/1, pp. 3–254.
[14] Barth, *The Knowledge of God and the Service of God*, Charles Scribner's Sons, New York, 1939, p. 7.

Whereupon Barth, with nary another reference to natural theology, devoted the remaining nineteen and a half lectures to a running commentary on the Scots Confession of 1560.

Why this ongoing repudiation of knowledge of God apart from Christian revelation? There are both theological and historical reasons for this, and one of the latter, while not decisive, furnishes a good starting point. All of Barth's fears about what happens when men reason from themselves to God were confirmed by what happened in Germany in the thirties. The "German Christians" found it possible to start with natural theology and move easily and comfortably to an acceptance of Adolf Hitler and the Nazi party as expressing God's will in their own day, since they had no criterion drawn from revelation by which to judge the rightness or wrongness of their assessment of Hitler. It was clear to Barth that when one judged all of God's work in the light of his revelation in Jesus Christ, no peace could be made with Hitler. Nazism, with its anti-Semitism and its exaltation of the Aryan race, was a repudiation of the gospel as understood in the light of Christian revelation. That those who started with natural theology ended with Hitler furnished final corroboration, if such were needed, of its falsity.

A good deal of the church struggle in the thirties, therefore, had to be theological as well as historical and sociological. This is why the famous Barmen Confession, in which the church expressed the basis of its opposition to Hitler, begins theologically:

Jesus Christ, as he is attested for us in Holy Scripture, is the one Word of God which we have to hear and which we have to trust and obey in life and in death.

We reject the false doctrine, as though the Church could and would have to acknowledge as a source of its proclamation, apart from and besides this one Word of God, still other events and powers, figures and truths, as God's revelation.[15]

15 Cited in Cochrane, *op. cit.*, p. 239.

The first paragraph explicitly asserts that there is but *one* source of our knowledge of God, Jesus Christ, while the second paragraph includes explicit repudiation of *any other* source of revelation, whether the "events and powers" be Hitler, Nazism, or—if we were to extend the principle to our own situation today—the American way of life.

But more is involved in the repudiation of natural theology than repudiation because of its political consequences. Perhaps the simplest way to state Barth's concern would be to put it like this: those who insist on finding God first in nature, or religious consciousness, or general history, or other religions, or whatever, are simply being ungrateful. If God has, in fact, given us the definitive and decisive revelation of himself in Jesus Christ, surely that is where we are first of all called upon to see him at work, and to be unwilling to do so is merely to demonstrate our ingratitude for this gift of himself that God has given us. Furthermore, when we insist on some form of natural theology, we are refusing to give Jesus Christ honor; we are demanding that he fit into the criteria by means of which we have independently determined how God shall act in revealing himself. This is arrogance, presumption and human pride. No, since God has made himself known in Jesus Christ we must start with that fact, and see every other fact in the light of it. He stands judge over all other presumed revelations, not they over him. If we reverse the order, as natural theology does, we make something else more ultimate than Jesus Christ, and try to fit him into a mold of our devising:

Who God is and what it is to be divine is something we have to learn where God has revealed Himself and His nature, the essence of the divine. And if He has revealed Himself in Jesus Christ as the God who does this, it is not for us to be wiser than He and to say that it is in contradiction with the divine essence. We have to be ready to be taught by Him that we have been too small and perverted in our thinking about Him within the framework of a false idea of God. It is not for us to speak of a contradiction and rift in the being of God, but to learn to correct our notions of the being of God, to reconstitute them in the light of the fact that He does this. . . . We cannot make [our insights] the standard by which to measure what God can or cannot do.[16]

Thus the rejection of natural theology is not an attempt to be theologically stubborn, but an attempt to be theologically honest, to let God meet us on his own terms. There is no clear path from man to God; such a path (represented by religion) only deifies man, only leads him to assume that the concept of "God" is of his own devising—the concept of "man" shouted loudly, in capital letters or italics. But there *is* a clear path from God to man, the path taken by God himself in condescending to stoop down to us, in humbling himself by identifying himself with us in Jesus Christ. Once we see what he was doing in Jesus Christ, we can see more clearly what he is doing everywhere else, but the order of priority is crucial.

This is why Barth is so critical of the Roman Catholic doctrine of the *analogia entis*, the analogy of being.[17] He feels that it is theologically disastrous to begin with the observation of various kinds of created beings, and on that basis advance to speak analogously of uncreated being, moving from observations about man to observations about God. To do this removes any real sense of distinction between God and man, since they are merely at different points on a continuum of being; it "partitions" God, making part of him knowable independently of revelation and the rest knowable only by revelation, and is thus only a particularized form of the basic sin of natural theology.[18]

Catholic critics have taken Barth much to task for what they feel are his one-sided misunderstandings of the doctrine,[19] but our present concern is not to argue the rights

[16] *Church Dogmatics*, IV/1, p. 186.
[17] Cf. particularly *Church Dogmatics*, I/1, where Barth refers to it as "the invention of Antichrist."
[18] Cf. the extended critique in *Church Dogmatics*, II/1, pp. 79ff.
[19] Cf. especially Henri Bouillard, *Karl Barth, Parole de Dieu et Existence Humaine*, deuxième partie, Aubier, Paris, 1957, pp. 190–217.

and wrongs of that particular debate. What is our concern is to see that although Barth rejects the notion of the analogy of being, he does not for a moment reject the notion of analogy. He sees, with other theologians, that language about God cannot be univocal, i.e., the words we use about God will not be identical in meaning with the words we use about man, or we would have obliterated the distinction between God and man. Nor can such language be equivocal, i.e., the words we use about God will not have totally different meanings from the words we use about man, or no speech about God would be intelligible. Consequently, language about God will be analogical, i.e., there will be *some* sense in which the same words can be used about both God and man, even though the similarity will be a similarity with a difference. Barth's use of analogies in speaking of God is—if we may oversimplify—precisely the *reverse* of the procedure employed in the analogy of being. We cannot, he says, look at man and derive conclusions about God. But we can look at God (since he has revealed himself) and derive conclusions about man. This is the *analogia fidei*, the analogy of faith, in which God is the analogue and man the analogate. Because we know through revelation, for example, that God is Father, we can come to analogous conclusions about what human fatherhood should be.

Or, to take an example he develops in various parts of Volume III of the *Dogmatics*, we can also speak of the *analogia relationis*, the analogy of relationship. We need to ponder carefully the meaning of the statement: "So God created man in his own image, in the image of God he created him; male and female he created them." (Gen. 1:27) The latter portion of this verse has not received sufficient attention in Biblical exegesis, Barth feels, and following up on ideas suggested in Dietrich Bonhoeffer's *Creation and Fall*, he points out that the God we know in Biblical revelation is the triune God, a God for whom true relationship exists within the Godhead in the mutual indwelling of Father, Son and Holy Spirit. Thus to speak of man as made in the image of *this* God will never mean man in isolation but man in relationship. The full meaning of "man," then, involves "male and female." Man apart from relationship, of which "male and female" is the most adequate symbol, is not true man.[20] It is with God in his revelation that we start, and from that we learn not only of him but also of ourselves. But we start with him, not with ourselves.

What Barth is after in the whole discussion of natural theology is expressed pictorially in the famous Isenheim altarpiece of Grunewald, to which Barth has called repeated attention in his writings.[21] In the painting of the Nativity, God the Father is high above in the heavens. Below him on earth is the Christ child, a very human child with a very human mother who is gazing at him. To the left, separated by a screen, are a host of angels and human beings also gazing at the child. The child is gazing upward and sees God the Father directly. But the mother, the angels and all the rest see the light emanating from the Father *only* as it is reflected in the face of the child. He is their sole means of access to the Father, and no man cometh unto the Father but by Him.

One could almost say that the whole issue of natural theology is focused in this painting. Any god found elsewhere than in the face of Jesus Christ will not be the God of Christian revelation, but a human construct, an idol, who can only lead men astray. The true God cannot be seen elsewhere than in and through that same Jesus Christ. The task, then, of dogmatics, of the church, of Christian preaching, is not to lead men down the false path of natural theology, but to concentrate wholeheartedly and unashamedly on pointing to Jesus Christ—as John the Baptist, in another part of the Isenheim altarpiece, points with his elongated forefinger to the gruesome man upon the cross, asserting that there, precisely there, is the event in which the distance between man and God has been overcome, by God becoming man.

If there is in fact something definitive and final about the

[20] See especially *Church Dogmatics*, III/1, pp. 194–197, and III/2, pp. 323–324.
[21] For what follows, see *Church Dogmatics*, I/2, p. 125.

revelation of God in Christ—and it is hard to see how *Christian* affirmation can say otherwise—then the issues raised in Barth's discussion of natural theology can scarcely be ignored by those who take the Christian affirmation seriously. That natural theology exists, Barth does not doubt. Nor does he doubt that it will continue to exist. But it has no right, he claims, to exist *in the church*, and Christian proclamation must never delude itself or its hearers by relying upon it. Christian proclamation can only rely upon the way God has actually chosen to reveal himself, and that way is the way of the Word made flesh who dwelt among us, and in whose face, as we learn from one greater than Grunewald, we behold the glory as of the only begotten of the Father, full of grace and truth.

IV

The discussion of natural theology, and its counterpart in the definitive nature of the revelation in Christ, has already implied the central positive thrust of Barth's theology, what Hans Urs von Balthasar and others have called the "Christological concentration." Barth insists rigorously that Christian thinking must begin with Christ and not elsewhere.[22] As he surveys the history of doctrine, Barth concludes that failure at this point has been responsible for the major Christian heresies, whether they be the Catholic doctrine of the *analogia entis* or the Reformed doctrine of election in its grotesque Calvinist form. If one is to isolate a single thing that Barth has done irrevocably to theology, it must surely be this rigorous insistence that Christ does not enter at the end of the human quest to add a final blessing to it, but that he must be present at the very beginning to determine the direction and content of all that follows.

[22] The basic formulation of Christology as a key to theological method is worked out in Barth's *Anselm: Fides Quaerens Intellectum*, John Knox Press, Richmond, Virginia, 1960.

Much does follow from this "Christological concentration," the full import of which in the *Dogmatics* itself can best be seen in the early part of IV/1, where Barth sets out the scheme to be followed throughout the rest of that volume (now four "part-volumes" strong, with a fifth still to appear). But from the whole of Barth's thought at least four positive emphases emerge as part of his legacy to future theologians, emphases that are particularly relevant to the American scene:

1. Above all, Barth emerges as the theologian of the *good news*, the man who has placed the gospel of grace squarely in the center of Christian affirmation. In what the present writer firmly believes to be the greatest single line in the whole twelve volumes, Barth asserts that God deals with man "not with a natural Therefore, but with a miraculous Nevertheless."[23] The sequence is not "Man is unworthy, *therefore* God rejects him," but rather "Man is unworthy, *nevertheless* God elects him." This is why man can hope, why he can believe, why he can trust in God.

Not only in Barth's sermons, where one would expect it, but in the *Dogmatics* as well, there are countless passages that breathe the most positive kind of affirmation of the goodness and wonder and power of God's overwhelming love. The gospel is not the mystery of incomprehensible darkness (as it has so often been for the orthodox) but the mystery of incomprehensible light.[24] It is not that we see so little of what God has done that we are puzzled, but that in the light of his revelation in Christ we see so much of what God has done that we are dazzled. One reads certain theologians and feels that they salvage so little from the New Testament that it does not really make much difference; one reads Barth and realizes that this man really believes that the most crucial event in all human history has really taken place, that God

[23] *Church Dogmatics*, II/2, p. 315.
[24] Compare Calvin's comments on the "horrible decree" with Barth's joyous affirmation in *Church Dogmatics*, II/2, pp. 146–155.

has really visited his people, that he has really redeemed his world, and that as a result everything is really different. Speaking of the doctrine of election, long the *bête noire* of those who nevertheless want to talk about the love and mercy of God, Barth affirms:

> It is not a mixed message of joy and terror, salvation and damnation. Originally and finally it is not dialectical but non-dialectical. It does not proclaim in the same breath both good and evil, both help and destruction, both life and death. It does, of course, throw a shadow. We cannot overlook or ignore this aspect of the matter. In itself, however, it is light and not darkness. . . . The Yes cannot be heard unless the No is also heard. But the No is said for the sake of the Yes and not for its own sake. In substance, therefore, the first and last word is Yes and not No . . .
>
> The election of grace is the sum of the Gospel—we must put it as pointedly as that. But more, the election of grace is the whole of the Gospel, the Gospel *in nuce*.[25]

Barth did not come to this conclusion in isolation from the real world but during the very years of the Hitlerian torment, when he was affirming with infectious assurance that this is still God's world, that his purposes cannot finally be thwarted, that the created world is the arena of his saving activity, and that come what may, the conviction that "Jesus is Victor," the guarantor of and witness to our salvation, is a conviction in the light of which we can face life or death, success or martyrdom, in serenity and confidence.[26]

[25] *Ibid.*, II/2, pp. 13–14.
[26] The relationship between Barth's confidence in what God is doing in the world and the very bleak character of that same world when viewed through faithless eyes, was brought home to the present writer during a period when he was reading, concurrently, III/1 of the *Dogmatics*, on creation, and Alan Bullock's *Hitler* (Harper and Brothers, New York, 1958). Everything being described in the latter book *seemed* to destroy the affirmations being made in the former book, until the writer realized that the book on creation had been written during, and in full consciousness of, the very events of World War II that Bullock describes so vividly. It became clear that it was the present writer's perspective, rather than Barth's, that was faulty.

To believe in grace, as Barth does, means to be thankful, for grace is undeserved blessing, unmerited gift, which we can never deserve but only receive thankfully.

Charis always demands the answer of *eucharistia* [i.e., grace always demands the answer of gratitude]. Grace and gratitude belong together like heaven and earth. Grace evokes gratitude like the voice an echo. Gratitude follows grace like thunder [follows] lightning.[27]

All we can really do, in the face of the gospel, is to be grateful. To be grateful is to be willing to receive a gift and to want to share that gift so that others can be grateful too. As one reads Barth, he realizes why the Christian faith has spread across the world: when people believe this sort of thing they have no alternative but to share it. Good news is not private. Nor is it news for a small elite, but for all, and therefore to be shared with all. Many conservative theologians criticize Barth for tending toward universalism, a belief that in the ultimate providence of God all men will be saved. Such men seem to need the reassurance of believing that other men (not themselves, but other men) will be damned. While Barth refuses to affirm an unequivocal universalism, for the very good reason that he has no more right to insist that God *must* save all people than the older theology had to insist that God *must* damn most people, he finds it strange that Christians should be so upset at the notion that God's good purposes for all his children should finally be achieved. "Peculiar Christendom," he apostrophizes, "whose most pressing problem seems to consist in this, that God's grace in this direction should be too free, that hell, instead of being amply populated, might one day perhaps be found to be empty."[28]

Because grace evokes gratitude, because good news must be shared, Barth's theology is a preacher's theology. This does not mean a theology reserved for preachers, but a theology

27 *Church Dogmatics*, IV/1, p. 41.
28 Barth, *Die Botschaft von der freien Gnade Gottes* (*Theologische Studien*, Heft 23), Evangelischer Verlag AG, Zollikon-Zürich, 1947, p. 8.

that can be preached. It cries out to be cried out. It is not an academic or speculative description of "someone else." It is the reader who is addressed, even on the printed page of scholarly dogmatics. In the midst of his treatment of the promise of election, Barth inserts this typical comment:

> The promise says to those who hear or read it: Thou mayest not hear or read at this point something said about another. Thou art not in the audience, but in the centre of the stage. This is meant for thee. Thou art "this" individual. Thou art isolated from God, and therefore a godless man. Thou art threatened. And yet thou standest indeed under a wholly new determination. It was for thee that Jesus Christ Himself bore the divine rejection in its real and terrible consequences. Thou art the one who has been spared from enduring it. And it is for thee that Jesus Christ is the elect man of God and arrayed in the divine glory. Eternal life and fellowship with God await thee. Jesus Christ died and rose for thee. It is thou who art elect with Him and through Him.[29]

2. A second important contribution of Barth has been his *incorporation of ethics into dogmatics*. If he will not settle for an ethic divorced from theology, no more will he settle for a theology divorced from ethics. The usual custom in large works of systematic theology or dogmatics, particularly of the continental variety, has been to set forth a full theological system and then leave to others the task of drawing ethical implications from it. Barth will have none of this. Ethics is not an appendage to dogmatics which can be treated by someone else when the dogmatic task has been completed. Rather, ethics must be incorporated into dogmatics all along the way, within the very heart of the structure.[30]

"Dogmatics has no option," Barth claims, "it has to be ethics as well. . . . Dogmatics itself is ethics; and ethics is also dogmatics. If this is understood as a fact, there is no danger that dogmatics may be dissolved in ethics, or a Chris-

[29] *Church Dogmatics*, II/2, p. 324.
[30] The basic setting forth of this position is in *Church Dogmatics*, II/2, pp. 782–796, "Dogmatics as Ethics."

tian existentialist philosophy. . . . Our task, then, is to include ethics within dogmatics."[31] Thus in Volume II, Barth turns from the Christian claim about the election of God (Chapter VII) to an immediate consideration of the command of God (Chapter VIII), and devotes the last three hundred pages of II/2 to an examination of the notion that the command is the claim, decision and judgment of God. In like manner, at the end of Volume III, he devotes an entire "part-volume" (III/4) to problems of ethics that emerge from a doctrine of creation, dealing specifically with such matters as war, suicide, love of neighbor, and vocation. The last part of Volume IV (IV/4) will deal with ethics as they emerge from a consideration of the doctrine of reconciliation.[32] The latter part of Volume V will presumably develop a similar ethic of redemption.

It is this stubborn refusal to permit ethics to get shunted off by itself and (perhaps more important) this even more stubborn refusal to permit dogmatics to exist in an ethical vacuum, that account for the activism of Barth's life and writing. During the thirties and the forties he was turning out huge volumes of the *Dogmatics* with his right hand while dashing off political tracts with his left—and in every case the left hand knew what the right was doing, and *vice versa*. M. Casalis' analysis of Barth's political writings underlines the conviction that theology and politics are closely wedded in Barth's mind, life and theology.

3. A third contribution that should be of particular value to Americans is *Barth's approach to the problem of tradition*.[33] Americans are liable to give short shrift to tradition and to insist that the Christian posture must be forward-looking

---

[31] *Ibid.*, pp. 793-794.

[32] Here, incidentally, will emerge one of the most controversial areas of Barth's theology. He has several times postponed his treatment of the sacraments, and now promises that they will be considered in IV/4 under ethics, as man's response to God's action—an approach as novel as it will be controversial to those who look upon the indissolubility of Word and Sacrament as a basic part of the Reformation heritage.

[33] The fullest treatment is in *Church Dogmatics*, I/2, pp. 538-660, "Authority in the Church." See also scattered passages in *The Knowledge of God and the Service of God*, and *Credo*.

rather than backward-looking. But the nature of the Christian faith is such that it is first of all a backward look—back to the revelation in Jesus Christ—so that what was true then can be appropriated in such fashion that it becomes true once again today. The matter is complicated by the fact that our knowledge of what happened "back then" is not mediated to us directly, but through the instrumentalities of Scripture and church, neither of which can be eliminated.

In discerning the gospel we are to preach, Barth insists that we go back finally to Scripture, but, more precisely, not *to* Scripture so much as *through* Scripture to the events of which Scripture itself is only the witness.

The fact that the primary sign of revelation, the existence of the prophets and apostles, is for the Church book and letter, does not rob it of its force as witness. If the book rises and the letter speaks, if the book is read and the letter understood, then with them the prophets and apostles and He of whom they testify rise up and meet the Church in a living way. *It is not the book and letter, but the voice of the men apprehended through the book and letter, and in the voice of these men the voice of Him who called them to speak, which is authority in the Church.*[34]

But we can recover the message of Scripture only through the church and hear the voice of Scripture only through the ears of the church. The problem, then, is the relation of Scripture and church. We cannot let the church be normative over Scripture (which is how Protestants incline to view the Roman Catholic answer to this problem), but must insist that the church remain *under* Scripture. We view Scripture through the church, for it has reflected upon the message of Scripture for nineteen centuries both in its confessional statements and in the writings of the church fathers. We may not always agree with them, but not until we have listened to them carefully can we be so presumptuous as to disagree.

[34] *Church Dogmatics*, I/2, p. 581, italics added.

To my mind, the whole question of tradition falls under the Fifth Commandment: Honour father and mother! Certainly that is a limited authority; we have to obey God more than father and mother. But we have also to obey father and mother. . . . There is no question of bondage and constraint. It is merely that in the church the same kind of obedience as, I hope, you pay to your father and mother, is demanded of you towards the Church's past, towards the "elders" of the Church.[35]

And if and when we do disagree with the elders, it will not be because of glorified hunches on our part, but because we have heard—perhaps with their help—a new word from Scripture that speaks with greater authority than they.

The norm that determines our choice is Holy Scripture. Holy Scripture is the object of our study, and at the same time the criterion of our study, of the Church's past. As I read the writings of the "Fathers," the witness of Holy Scripture stands continually before my eyes; I accept what interprets this witness to me; I reject what contradicts it. So a choice is actually made, certainly not a choice according to my individual taste, but according to my knowledge of Holy Scripture.[36]

The classic example of Barth's willingness to follow his own logic in the matter occurs in his treatment of election. Introducing his treatment of the subject in II/2, he wrote retrospectively in the preface:

To think of the contents of this volume gives me much pleasure, but even greater anxiety. The work has this peculiarity, that in it I have had to leave the framework of theological tradition to a far greater degree than in the first part on the doctrine of God. I would have preferred to follow Calvin's doctrine of predestination much more closely, instead of departing from it so radically. . . . But I could not and cannot do so. *As I let the Bible itself speak to me on these matters, as I meditated upon what I seemed to hear, I was driven irresistibly to reconstruction.* . . . It is be-

35 *Credo*, Charles Scribner's Sons (The Scribner Library), New York, 1962, p. 181.
36 *Ibid.*, p. 183.

cause of the rather critical nature of the case that I have had to introduce into this half-volume such long expositions of some Old and New Testament passages.[37]

Here is the key to the matter. The obligation of a theologian is to listen to the tradition as it meditates on Scripture. But, when tradition (in this case, Calvin) and Scripture speak a different language, there is no doubt where the priority must lie. It must lie with Scripture. If tradition helps to illumine what Scripture tells us, it is to be employed gratefully. But if it clashes with Scripture, it must be challenged. And so Barth, hearing the New Testament speak in hopeful terms about God's election of man in Jesus Christ, parts company with Calvin because he feels that at this point Calvin did not stay with the Biblical witness.

This willingness to take issue with tradition—but only after one has gratefully appropriated from it—means that there is a very radical side to Barth's thought. It is radical not so much in the sense of being brand new (though it is often that), but radical in the sense that it tries to get at the root (*radix*) of the matter and then start afresh, letting the theological chips fall where they may. If one is right in the root starting point, then one can proceed with confidence, even though the new way seems strange. The root of the matter is the gospel, preserved in Scripture, attesting to what God has done in Jesus Christ. The Reformers got into such difficulty on the issue of pre-destination simply because *at this point*, unaccountably, they did not listen to Scripture in the same manner that they had listened to Scripture at other points. Rather than beginning with the God made known in Jesus Christ, they began with a deity describable by such abstract terms as omnipotence and omniscience. They committed the cardinal theological error of proceeding from the abstract to the concrete, rather than the other way around.[38] But the God to whom the Bible witnesses is not an abstract deity; he is the living Lord who is

---

[37] *Church Dogmatics*, II/2, p. x, italics added.
[38] On this point cf. *Church Dogmatics*, II/2, pp. 51–76.

the God of Abraham, Isaac and Jacob, and also the God and Father of our Lord Jesus Christ. *He* is the electing God, and all that we affirm about his good pleasure toward man in and through the sending of Jesus Christ must be based on the God *He* is—the God who is for man and not against him. If this is true, the consequences, however daring and unexpected, may not be shunned. In Barth's case they lead him to a whole new way of understanding man's status before God.

Concern for Scripture and tradition do not, in other words, lead to bondage but to an unparalleled degree of theological freedom that comes precisely at the moment when, paradoxically, one binds himself to the Biblical revelation. In such bondage one becomes free to hear the clear, unfettered word of the gospel, and to break out of the logical straitjackets that have been devised not by God but by his well-meaning if ill-advised servants.

4. Lest all this sound as though Christians are called upon to set up a closed shop and banish non-union members from their sight, we must point to a final contribution that Barth makes to the American situation, particularly to the American situation of religious pluralism. This is *his treatment of the "others,"* the so-called nonbelievers, who do not share the profession of faith of Christians. Who are they, really? How do they stand before God? And how, consequently, do they stand in relation to us?

Our comments on Barth's treatment of election have already made plain that there is no vantage point from which the Christian can gloat over the "others" as though he had been given something denied to them and thus stood above them. God has declared himself for men, and this means *all* men, not just the tiny handful who happen to be within the church. This means that the basic difference between Christian and non-Christian is not that the Christian is saved, while the non-Christian is damned, but that the Christian knows what the true situation of all men is, i.e., what God's intention for them is, whereas the non-Christian does not. The most the non-Christian can do is to live a lie, i.e., to live a life that contradicts God's already declared intention for him. He can live, in other words, *as though* he were not one of the elect, though *in fact* God wills that he shall be of the elect. The most he can do is to show forth the nature of that from which God has already willed to save him.

On the face of it, this sounds as though God had over-ruled man's freedom, but Barth makes clear that such is not the case:

Man can certainly keep on lying (and does so); but he cannot make truth falsehood. He can certainly rebel (he does so); but he can accomplish nothing which abolishes the choice of God. He can certainly flee from God (he does so); but he cannot escape Him. He can certainly hate God and be hateful to God (he does and is so); but he cannot change into its opposite the eternal love of God which triumphs even in His hate. He can certainly give himself to isolation (he does so—he thinks, wills and behaves god-lessly, and is godless); but even in his isolation he must demon-strate that which he wishes to controvert—the impossibility of play-ing the "individual" over against God. He may let go of God, but God does not let go of him.[39]

Thus the "others." The elect, for their part, are called . . . to what? Not to glory in their election, but to acquaint the "others" with the fact that they too are the objects of God's grace, and that they are rejected only in the sense of "rejected men *elected*," men to whom God's grace has already reached out, and who are now called upon to acknowledge this fact and live a life of truth rather than falsehood. The task of the elect is thus to effect what Barth calls "frontier crossings" be-tween the kingdom of darkness and the kingdom of light.[40]

The Christian, then, can never approach the non-Christian as one who stands beneath him, to whom the Christian, out of the largesse of his bounty, will stoop. No, Christian and non-Christian stand side by side in their common need and

[39] *Church Dogmatics*, II/2, p. 317.
[40] Cf. further on this point *ibid.*, II/2, pp. 410–419, and 449–458.

their common humanity, united by the fact that they are both the ones to whom God himself has stooped.

Who is it who really has to stoop down at this point? Not one man to another, a believer to an unbeliever, as all natural theology fatally but inevitably supposes. He who stoops down to the level of us all, both believers and unbelievers, is the real God alone, in His grace and mercy. And it is only by the fact that he knows this that the believing man is distinguished from the unbeliever. Faith consists precisely in this—in the life which is lived in consequence of God's coming down to our level.[41]

This disposes of the arrogant Christian, that unlovely missioner who says in effect, "I'm saved and if you'll do as I say, I'll condescend to arrange for you to be saved too." It also disposes of the indifferent Christian, that unexcited and unexciting pallid believer who is so afraid of being called arrogant that he leaves the sharing of the gospel as a matter of extreme indifference. Actually it is a matter of extreme importance, but since all is of grace no one can lord it over the other. He can only try to share what he has mysteriously been given, sure that no limits can be placed around its transforming possibilities: "No man who has himself received the testimony of Jesus Christ will agree that it is in principle inaccessible for any other man."[42] The "other" is "the man whose offense is so great that there neither is nor can there be conceived anything greater—except the compassion of God."[43]

V

So much for some emphases in Barth's thought that are particularly relevant to the American scene. But one does no honor to Barth merely by praising him. He is not on the scene

[41] *Ibid.*, II/1, p. 95.
[42] *Church Dogmatics*, II/2, p. 350.
[43] *Ibid.*, II/2, p. 445.

to end the dialogue among Christians by training a chorus that will chant a Barthian monologue; he is on the scene precisely to ensure that the dialogue continues. It is therefore important to criticize as well as to commend. In the present case the critique will be brief, to illustrate the point that Americans must listen and absorb before they start to demolish. We have already suggested that many American criticisms of Barth have been based on misinformation, and we now suggest that it will be a long time before most Americans are familiar enough with Barth's theology to be able to offer *responsible* criticism. But criticism there must be if we are to avoid making a golden calf at the end of our pilgrimage to this particular Sinai.[44]

The following are typical of the kinds of questions that are most frequently raised when Barth's theology is under discussion. They are not of equal weight and seriousness, but they indicate areas of Barth's thought in which theologians of varying persuasions have been less than fully satisfied.

1. The center of Barth's theological method, the "Christological concentration," has often been the subject of questions. Does this not take one aspect of the gospel, admittedly the central one, and overinflate it to the point where practically everything else is eliminated? Is the Old Testament, for example, as centrally a book about Christ as Barth's exegesis would seem to suggest? Must it not be read on its own terms, and not merely through Christian eyes? Does not Barth's insistence on viewing election Christologically downgrade the

[44] It is not a criticism but a description of M. Casalis' book to say that it is uncritical. One cannot, after all, do everything in a hundred pages. At some points, another writer might want to temper the estimate. That Barth is consistently fair to his theological opponents is less clear, for example, in his "Angry Introduction" to *Nein!* (the reply to Emil Brunner in *Natural Theology*, Geoffrey Bles, London, 1946) and in some of his comments about Reinhold Niebuhr, than it is in *Protestant Thought: from Rousseau to Ritschl* (Harper and Brothers, New York, 1959). Barth seems, in fact, to treat dead theologians with much greater respect than living ones. And as already suggested, the notion that Barth's historical judgments are unfailingly right is challenged by Roman Catholic theologians who have criticized his treatment of the *analogia entis*.

emphasis on judgment that is undeniably to be found in the Bible? Does he not have to engage in special pleading to remove natural theology from the Bible, or to reverse the traditional relationship of Christ and Adam?

2. With the overwhelming emphasis on "the triumph of grace," or (as Barth now prefers) the stress on "Jesus as victor," is there a consistently worked out place for true human freedom? Barth insists that there is, and "freedom" becomes a key word in later volumes of the *Dogmatics*. But is not man's freedom to rebel, for example, in any ultimate sense, seriously limited by the overpowering nature of the grace that is directed toward him? Is there not a danger that, as John Bennett and others have put it, man is "swamped by grace" in Barth's theology?[45]

3. Is Barth's radical dependence on Scripture really possible in our day without more extensive exploration of problems raised by the breakdown of verbal inerrancy, the presupposition in terms of which the Reformers defended the sufficiency of Scripture in the first place? Is it possible (and this is a question all Protestants along with Barth must face) for contemporary emphasis on the authority of Scripture to escape the charge that dependence on Scripture is dependence on the individual's own interpretation of the particular parts of Scripture to which he is willing to listen?[46]

4. On what terms are discriminating judgments possible between various levels within Scripture? Barth, for example, treats the creation stories as "sagas," different in kind from the "history" found elsewhere in the Old Testament. But this distinction is not employed in the New Testament, where claims about the virgin birth are defended in a much more literalistic way. By means of what criteria are such distinctions maintained?

[45] Cf. further on this point the issues raised by G. C. Berkouwer in *The Triumph of Grace in the Theology of Karl Barth*, William B. Eerdmans Publishing Company, Grand Rapids, Michigan, 1956.
[46] This is a widely expressed Roman Catholic criticism. Cf. *inter alia* Jerome Hamer, O.P., *Karl Barth*, Newman Press, Westminster, Maryland, 1962, especially pp. 101–102.

5. Does Barth grapple realistically enough with evil? He is so full of the New Testament claim that Christ is already victor over the powers of evil that there is really no place for evil to fit in his theology. Evil is an "ontological impossibility." It is nevertheless, though unaccountably, still with us. It shouldn't be, but it is! We must ask if evil is not much more oppressively with us than Barth's analysis can allow, and if it must not be given more status in any theology that claims to do justice to all dimensions of reality.

6. In what manner can a real connecting line be drawn between Barth's theological judgments and his ethical conclusions? If one feels that a given ethical or political decision of Barth's is naive or even irresponsible, as many have felt about his stand on communism, does this cast a judgment on the theology that has led to such a decision, or is it merely to be understood as a fallible human judgment with which one can disagree, quite apart from the theology that inspired it? It has been the burden of much of Reinhold Niebuhr's criticism of Barth, for example, that if his theology leads to the political conclusions Barth espouses, it is thereby rendered suspect--a critique, it must be added, not unlike one level of Barth's attack on the "German Christians."[47]

7. Are there not specific areas where Barth, for the sake of the symmetry of the system, has done less than justice to his subject matter? His treatment of the Jews, for example, in II/2, fits well into a systematic statement, but one wonders whether it represents a description of any actual Jew, and whether the notion of "Israel" in that section has not become an abstract theological concept rather than the description of a living, flesh-and-blood group of real people. Similarly, there has been criticism of his doctrine of election on the

[47] See Reinhold Niebuhr, *Essays in Applied Christianity*, Meridian Books, New York, 1959. The most thorough interpretations of Barth's political ethics are Charles West, *Communism and the Theologians*, Westminster Press, Philadelphia, 1958, pp. 177–326, and Will Herberg, "The Social Philosophy of Karl Barth," an introduction to Barth, *Community, State, and Church*, Doubleday and Company (Anchor Books), Garden City, New York, 1960, pp. 11–67.

grounds that it leads to conclusions incompatible with the totality of the Biblical witness.[48] It is already clear that with the appearance of IV/4, Barth's novel treatment of the sacraments will need critical analysis.

8. There is a real problem in the area of Christian communication. To what degree can Barth's approach make contact with the person who does not accept all the presuppositions on which it is based? Must not one already believe before he can hear what Barth has to say? Is there not a danger that his theology will be a source of truth only to those already committed, and that others will have to be won to the faith by apologetic tools less pure, perhaps even by the use of natural theology? Until one stands within the circle of faith Barth has circumscribed, can he really hear? May this not become a theology of the elite?

Other questions could be raised.[49] The above, however, are among the questions most often raised. Barth has faced them all at one point or another in his writings, and answered them at least to his own satisfaction and that of his followers. But an interesting thing should be noted in relation to criticisms of Barth. Many, perhaps most, of them arise out of the fact that for Barth the gospel is so unambiguously and so wonderfully the goods news. Most theologians of the past have come in for criticism because they made the Christian message too parochial, and described it from a perspective that their critics felt was confining rather than liberating. Most of Barth's problems, at any rate, are raised because he gives such total credence to all that is joyous and liberating in the Christian message. It may be a good thing for Christendom to have

[48] Emil Brunner has been particularly restive about Barth's conclusions in this area. Cf. Brunner, *The Christian Doctrine of God*, Westminster Press, Philadelphia, 1950, Chapters 22–23, and also G. F. Hendry's able critique of II/2, in *Theology Today*, October 1958, pp. 396–404.

[49] See, for example, the Lutheran critique of Barth in Gustaf Wingren, *Theology in Conflict*, Muhlenberg Press, Philadelphia, 1958, especially Chapters 2 and 6, and the orthodox Calvinist critique in Fred H. Klooster, *The Significance of Barth's Theology*, Baker Book House, Grand Rapids, Michigan, 1961.

to deal for awhile with problems arising out of a generous view of the gospel, rather than having to defend itself against charges that are leveled because it cannot set its sights sufficiently high.

VI

The dialogue between Barth and the rest of the theological world will continue. We must reckon with the fact that the end is not yet. There are more volumes to come, and there may be more surprises in store. We have no way of knowing where Barth will end, and we may be sure that he does not know either. For as he has said, when he begins work on a new volume only the angels know what that volume will contain. It may be that the angels know what is in IV/4 and V, although we do not. But apparently we will have to wait, for the angels seem reluctant to tell us. It may be, as Barth has whimsically suggested in another connection, that they are too busy playing Mozart.

PART ONE ⟶⟨⟩⟵

Introduction

Not since Luther and Calvin has Protestantism had a single theologian of the stature and importance of Karl Barth. He is moreover one of those few men within a given period of history who make such an impact in their own sphere of influence that a new epoch begins with them; even their adversaries are only important in relation to them. The Reformed churches have been so utterly shaken by Barth's message, and the reverberations of his work within those churches have been so far-reaching, that they have not yet adjusted themselves to the new situation. Like a patient who recovers his health very slowly after a critical operation, they are incapable of analyzing what has happened and of taking their bearings. Paradoxically—or perhaps very naturally if the comparison holds—those who are strangers to the Protestant ethos, for the most part Roman Catholics, have been much more concerned about Barth's impact and its implications. The list of works published by them is increasing all the time, and already includes a number of works of considerable importance, making clear that Barth is watched, listened to and understood with real penetration by those outside the circle of his own confession (he belongs to the Calvinist wing of the Reformed church), as well as by the larger group of churches coming from the Reformation itself.

Even though he conscientiously aligns himself with the particular tradition to which he belongs, Barth refuses to let himself be enclosed within any narrow framework. His theological perspective is thoroughly ecumenical, and the truth he seeks and proclaims is not the possession of any one church or theological clique. Furthermore, improbable as such a statement may sound, Barth is never concerned to defend the truth of a theological party line; rather it is Truth itself, one and universal, which he is humbly but boldly trying to receive and transmit.

This is why the Roman Catholic church listens to him and studies him with such respect. For many years in Basel an outstanding Roman Catholic theologian, Hans Urs von Balthasar, has been a lucid, critical and admiring witness to Barth's progress in the further uncovering of the Truth. If von Balthasar is right, not only is Protestantism renewed in the process, but the whole church is likewise affected—simultaneously shaken inside out and filled up again, radically challenged and profoundly renewed. Barth delineates a whole new vision for faith, life and Christian witness, and also for love, art, politics and the whole of human life as it is lived by the most diverse kinds of men, from the humblest to the richest and most cultured. Who can be indifferent?

Just because as Christians we may live in the truth of Jesus Christ and therefore in the light of the knowledge of God and therefore with an illumined reason, we shall also become sure of the meaning of our own existence and of the ground and goal of all that happens. Once more a quite tremendous extension of the field of vision is indicated by this; to know this object in its truth means in truth to know no more and no less than all things, even man, oneself, the cosmos, and the world. The truth of Jesus Christ is not one truth among others; it is *the* truth, the universal truth that creates all truth as surely as it is the truth of God, the *prima veritas* which is also the *ultima veritas*. For in Jesus Christ God has created all things, He has created all of us. We exist not apart from Him but in Him, borne by Him, the Almighty Word. To know Him is to know all.[1]

[1] Barth, *Dogmatics in Outline*, Harper and Brothers (Torchbooks), New York, 1959, p. 26.

Those who were present in 1948 at the opening session of the first assembly of the World Council of Churches at Amsterdam are not likely to forget the scene. There were between three and four thousand persons present, representing one hundred and fifty-one churches from forty-two different countries—everything from Old Catholics to Quakers. Present also were Queen Juliana and the Prince Consort of the Netherlands, John Foster Dulles and numerous Catholic observers, as well as world press representatives. Before this assembly, Barth was given the responsibility of introducing the central theme of the conference, "Man's Disorder and God's Design." And these are the words with which he challenged them:

May I begin by asking you to consider the question whether we must not view and handle this theme, as a whole and in all its aspects, in reverse order. It is written, we should *first* seek God's Kingdom and His righteousness, so that all we need in relation to the world's disorder may be added unto us. Do we not need, do we not want, to take this order of topics seriously? God's saving design is above—but the world's disorder, and therefore also our own conceptions of its causes, and therefore also our proposals and plans to combat it, are all *below*. What this whole lower realm (including our own churchly existence!) means, can only—if at all— become clear and understandable to us from above, from the perspective of God's design. Whereas from the world's disorder, and also from our Christian analyses and postulates applied to it, there is no view, no way that leads out and up to God's design.

We should not try in any of our sections to begin down below; neither with the unity and disunity of our churches, nor with the good and bad manners of modern man, nor with the terrifying picture of a culture which is only technically oriented and only concerned with production, nor with the clash between a godless West and a godless East, nor with the threat of the atomic bomb, and certainly not with the few considerations and measures by which we think we might cure all this calamity. In the material that lies before us there speak too many voices laden with repressed care and anxiety, and on the other hand too many voices expressive of all too fond illusions, for us not to need this warning. They are symptomatic of the fact that the question about the right order of procedure, which is from the top downward, is not a question that makes no difference.

We are certainly right when we try to put our brother the modern man on his guard against forgetting, in the presence of purely scientific and technical problems and solutions, that he himself is a part of the evil he thinks to overcome in this way, against forgetting that he is not judge but accused, against forgetting that human existence has no meaning without faith in a transcendent truth, goodness, and love which man himself has not created, and by which he can only let himself be bound. But how about the beam in our own eye, at all three of these points, and how could we then help this brother of ours, if we should enter upon and persist in a positivistic way of thinking, which would certainly have nothing to do with the *Christian* realism that is required of us?[2]

Turning the question about in this fashion, challenging all the work done before the conference, referring all Christians, both laymen and theologians, back to the gospel, Barth electrified the conference. Those present could not evade his question and were pushed by it to a seriousness, depth and examination of essentials which contributed greatly to deepening what was at that time the precarious unity of the churches gathered together in the ecumenical movement.

This extended illustration is included to indicate how Barth intervenes to make a point, unsettles accustomed patterns and opens up new lines of approach.

In 1954, at the time of the second assembly of the World Council of Churches held in Evanston, Illinois, Barth decided not to cross the Atlantic, for America has always been a strange and somewhat frightening place to him. He was nevertheless a faithful member of the "Advisory Commission on the Main Theme," and at many points the report of this commission shows the effect of Barth's pen. Here again his efforts bore real fruit.

But it is time to learn something about him.

[2] From the translation prepared for the English-speaking delegates at the Amsterdam Assembly.

PART TWO

The Direction of Barth's Life

Karl Barth was born in Basel, Switzerland, on May 10, 1886. His father, Fritz Barth, was a professor of theology in his own right, a specialist in the New Testament, about which he wrote an *Introduction* published in 1908 that is still useful today. In family background and indeed in all of his being, Barth is a "Baseler," and he exemplifies the characteristics of such a background, including a seriousness of mind and a depth of intelligence which, far from resting content with surface brilliance, probe with a sure instinct to the heart of any problem. To Barth, study, research and intellectual creativity are not impositions to be endured grudgingly and unhappily. On the contrary, he has a passion for just such things, so that his work is saturated with a love of learning, a curiosity, and a willingness to push ideas to their logical conclusion, that are little short of amazing.

A couple of examples can illustrate this. When he was still a young professor at Göttingen, Germany, he began the habit of writing out his lectures in full. (This is a habit, incidentally, that Barth has retained to the present day, and the material from his lectures is printed in full in the various volumes of the *Church Dogmatics*. But even the editing of these lectures is preceded by long, patient and implacable research in every area under examination.) Early in his teaching career, this preliminary work, in the course of which all sorts of problems had to be treated, often left Barth in a situation where the final editing was scarcely completed before the beginning of the lecture. One day he stopped lecturing after about twenty minutes, and said, "Gentlemen, due to the difficulty of today's subject matter, this is as far as I have gotten. We shall have to leave it at that. Class dismissed!"

Several years later he began to publish a *Dogmatics*. A huge *Prolegomena* appeared in 1927. Then, quite unexpectedly, in 1932, when the theological world was waiting for a new edition and a sequel, Barth began again from scratch, explaining in his preface that he did so out of respect for the truth:

> I could and I wanted to say the same thing as before; but now I could no longer say it in the way in which I had said it before. . . . During the five years every problem has assumed for me a very much richer, more mobile, and more difficult aspect. I had to make more extensive soundings and lay broader foundations. And now I still venture to hope that with it all everything has actually become simpler and clearer.[1]

From his native city, with its long tradition of humanist culture, Barth has inherited this extraordinary respect for the truth, this *Gründlichkeit*, as the Germans call it, which is unwilling to leave anything obscure. He has also inherited a professional conscientiousness that, once persuaded that university teaching is the noblest of human occupations and the highest responsibility a man can have, wishes to leave nothing to guesswork or improvisation. Words have seldom been more carefully thought out, more surely justified, more solidly supported than his. (Barth, incidentally, is not far from Plato at this point in thinking that the philosopher—rather, the theologian!—is the soul of the city.)

From Basel also, Barth received his critical clarity and his feeling for polemics. He illustrates perfectly the language of the Baselers, which is razor-sharp and rapid, with a penchant for irony and sharp repartee. The innumerable flashes of wit, the whimsy and the jokes that enliven his conversation, cor-

[1] Barth, *Church Dogmatics*, I/1, T. & T. Clark, Edinburgh, 1936, pp. vii–viii.

respondence and teaching, all witness to this. For this reason
he is both a remarkable teacher and a formidable speaker.
The theological debates in which he has been involved have
given him an opportunity to put these natural gifts, which
he clearly regards as assets, to use; and many of those who
have locked horns with him in theological combat acknowledge the superiority of his intellect and his incomparable culture, and they bow down before his unusual relevance.

Although he was born in Basel, Barth grew up in Bern, the
administrative capital of Switzerland, whose authority is always more or less under challenge from the various cantons of
the Swiss confederation. Barth has never felt much at home in
this rather conventional city. He enjoys spoofing the Bernese,
whose diplomatic authority he tolerates without enthusiasm,
and whose officials have more than once demonstrated the
suspicion any government feels toward those of its citizens
who accept no limitation to their freedom of thought and expression.

THEOLOGICAL STUDIES

Barth carried on his theological studies at the universities
of Bern, Berlin, Tübingen and Marburg, where he came to
know the Germany—even then threatening and alarming—
that was to play such an important role in his later life. His
professors were the great teachers of the theological liberalism
of the early twentieth century. One of these was Adolf
von Harnack (1851–1930), particularly famous for his *History of Dogma* (1886–1889) and his attempts to explain the
development of dogma in early Christianity as a Helleniza-
tion of the original message of Jesus. In Harnack's *What Is
Christianity?* (1900) it is not God in his revelation who is
at the center of the faith and piety of the church, but rather
believing man in relation to a divine being whose nature is
scarcely discernible. Thus Harnack exemplified the anthro-

pocentric tendency which, since Schleiermacher, had characterized Protestant liberalism.

Hermann Gunkel (1862–1932), another of Barth's teachers, represented the most radical historical-critical position, as it attempted to understand the Old Testament. He won considerable fame for his studies of the parallels between Babylonian and Biblical mythologies. Adolf Schlatter (1852–1938), on the other hand, while primarily a specialist in Judaism and New Testament criticism, offered a systematic and positive alternative to the prevailing historical criticism.

But the greatest influence on the young Barth was Wilhelm Herrmann (1846–1922), the most celebrated student of Ritschl, and the champion of a neo-Kantian dogmatics. Herrmann had a decisive influence on all those who studied with him, due both to his extraordinary ability as a teacher and to the authority of his remarkable personality. For Herrmann also, anthropology was at the center of personal life, and human problems could not be resolved apart from encounter with the living God. It was by contact with the inner life of Jesus, who had a perfect religious personality, that one's own personal religious life could be born and mature. A decisive religious experience is thus brought about by contact with an exceptional person, even though historical investigation cannot fully uncover what he was like nor fully communicate his real power.

It was as the faithful pupil of these teachers, particularly Herrmann, that Barth finished his university education. As one of their followers, he was prepared to be a theologian strictly dependent on the sole criterion of historical investigation, and a preacher whose message would be determined by the anthropological question of religious experience.

While he was still a student, Barth met Eduard Thurneysen and began a lifelong acquaintance with the friend who has ever since been his companion in the theological enterprise. The two of them shortly had occasion to go to Bad Boll, where they made the acquaintance of Christoph Blumhardt, the great preacher whose personality and message had such a decisive influence on both their personal lives and their theology. Son of the famous Johann Christoph Blumhardt, founder of the retreat center at Bad Boll in Württemberg, Christoph Blumhardt (1842–1919) was, like his father, an untiring preacher of the Kingdom of God. Like his father also, Christoph Blumhardt found the gospel and the strength needed for Christian living summarized in the phrase, "Jesus is Victor."[2] Solidly rooted in a vigorous pietist tradition, greatly invigorated by the eschatological renewal inaugurated by his father, Christoph Blumhardt was at the same time a man of broad cultural understanding, willing to face the questions posed by a modern science based on atheistic presuppositions, in the same way that he confronted socialism and its materialistic philosophy. At this point he was so identified with the working class that from 1900 to 1906 he was the deputy of the Social Democratic Party to the *Landtag* of Württemberg. In those days such action was considered little short of scandalous.

Later, Blumhardt acknowledged that this period of political involvement had convinced him of the absolute necessity of a spiritual transformation in man as preferable to a radical modification of social and political structures. This in turn led him to put renewed emphasis on strictly pastoral activity, more than ever centered on the objective reality of God and his Kingdom, and characterized by a simple Biblical faith. For Christoph Blumhardt as for his father also, Jesus, man *par excellence,* is the savior of the whole world, the one who by virtue of his divine power rules and defeats all the demonic powers. The universal love of God, incarnated and fulfilled in Jesus Christ, makes it impossible for us to assume that men's estrangement from God and their hostility to the message of salvation is final and definitive. The light of the

[2] Translator's Note: The lasting influence of Blumhardt on Barth can be measured by the fact that in *Church Dogmatics,* IV/3, Part 1, Barth devotes over a hundred pages to a contemporary elaboration of this theme, in the course of which he asserts that the phrase "Jesus is Victor" is a better summation of his theology than the phrase "the triumph of grace." See especially pp. 173–180.

resurrection, which is the world's true destiny even now, illumines the present, whatever obscurities may still remain.

Such is the teaching that reentrenched in the authentic evangelical line the theological liberal that Barth had become under the influence of his learned professors.

THE EPISTLE TO THE ROMANS

In 1909 Barth entered the service of the Swiss German Reformed parish of Geneva, where he developed a continuing love for the French language and culture, although the city itself, with its artificial atmosphere of an international and ecumenical metropolis, has always remained somewhat strange to him.

In 1911 he became pastor at Safenwil, a village in Aargau, where he spent ten decisive years maturing, thinking and working. As a pastor of what had originally been nothing but a rural parish, Barth had to face the social problems raised by the developing of an important industry, for the majority of his parishioners were factory workers. Like Blumhardt in Württemberg, and like the Christian Socialist Leonard Ragaz, whose teaching he appropriated eagerly, Barth frequently took stands in the conflicts between the workers and owners that were quickly labeled "socialist," but which in any case hardly conformed to the attitude traditionally expected of a Swiss pastor! He organized union activity and demanded wage increases for the workers. In 1915 he joined the Social Democratic Party.

But all of this, while important, was only secondary. For the thing to which he gave chief attention during the ten years at Safenwil was *preaching*: the problem of how to say what one has to say—but even more the problem of the content of the message that, Sunday after Sunday, must be delivered by one who has the heavy responsibility of entering the Christian pulpit to preach.

In this situation Barth began a program of Bible study,

which he intensified more than ever after the outbreak of World War I. Although protected by Swiss neutrality, Barth had neither the desire nor the will to be above the conflict. He felt intensely involved in the sudden shifts of battle, and particularly stressed that if preaching meant anything at all, it ought to be proclaimed in the midst of the explosion of bombs and the cries of the dying, not as a colorless and insipid message, timeless and unrelated to the basic spiritual questions that were thrust on all men by the outburst of war and its whole train of atrocities. Such times demanded a kind of preaching that would reconsider all these questions, listen to them and illumine them from a new perspective, placing them in a scale of objective values that would convey peace and courage and faith in God to the confused spirits of men, even when God's love seemed to be mocked by the course of events. Barth also felt that he must attack the false peace of the indifferent Swiss, denounce the egoism on which their ease and comfort were based, and likewise denounce the maneuverings of Bernese politics.

When many others were withdrawing into an ivory tower, Barth was participating in all that was going on in the world. He took advantage of the refuge in which he found himself so that he was more involved and more perceptive about what was going on than those who were in the midst of the battle itself. The following titles are indicative of the relatively few works printed during this period:[3] *Faith in a Personal God,* 1914 (41); *God's Vanguard,* 1915 (49); *The Justice of God,* 1916 (52); *The One Thing Necessary,* 1916 (53); *Waiting for the Kingdom of God,* 1916 (55); *On the Other Side of the Boarder,* 1917 (56); and *Seek God and You Shall Live,* 1918 (58).

[3] Translator's Note: Throughout this book, untranslated works by Barth will be cited with an English title and a reference number in parentheses. In each case the number identifies the work in the full bibliography prepared by Charlotte von Kirschbaum, found in the *Festschrift* prepared for Barth's seventieth birthday, *Antwort,* Evangelischer Verlag AG, Zollikon-Zürich, 1956, pp. 945–960. Works of Barth available in English will be cited in the most recent English edition available.

Once again it was the Bible that was the touchstone for his thinking and inquiry throughout this period of world upheaval and national revolutions. Eduard Thurneysen was also pastor in a town not many miles from Barth, on the other side of the hill, and the two friends explored the faith together, writing each other and meeting together, exchanging their discoveries and sharing their confusions. As a result of all this, the pages of a huge work slowly accumulated at Safenwil—a Biblical commentary, an existential outburst, and an impassioned interpretation of *The Epistle to the Romans*. Once again St. Paul's great letter became the source of a spiritual pilgrimage that profoundly altered Christendom. The huge commentary, which had five hundred pages in small print, appeared in 1919. Barth wrote in the preface:

Paul, as a child of his age, addressed his contemporaries. It is, however, far more important that, as Prophet and Apostle of the Kingdom of God, he veritably speak to all men of every age. . . . If we rightly understand ourselves, our problems are the problems of Paul; and if we be enlightened by the brightness of his answers, those answers must be ours . . .

It is certain that in the past men who hungered and thirsted after righteousness naturally recognized that they were bound to labour with Paul. They could not remain unmoved spectators in his presence. Perhaps we too are entering upon such a time.[4]

Throughout the theological world, but particularly in Protestant Germany, the work aroused great interest and violent reactions. Writing later about the impact that his *Romans* had made, Barth commented:

As I look back upon my course, I seem to myself as one who, ascending the dark staircase of a church tower and trying to steady himself, reached for the banister, but got hold of the bell rope in-

[4] Preface to the first edition of Barth, *The Epistle to the Romans*, Oxford University Press, London, 1933, p. 1.

stead. To his horror, he had then to listen to what the great bell had sounded over him and not over him alone.[5]

A second edition, taking account of the reactions, some of which were grateful and some of which were furious, was published in Munich in 1922. It was another bombshell, and over twenty-five thousand copies have been published up to the present time.

In the meantime Barth had left Safenwil, and accepting the call of the Reformed church of eastern Friesland, he became Honorary Professor of Reformed Theology, after the University of Göttingen agreed to the establishment of a chair devoted to this subject which was created and endowed by a substantial gift from the Presbyterian Church in the United States of America. From this time on, Barth's profession, his vocation and his total concern are centered on being a professor of dogmatics or systematic theology. Before all else Barth is a theologian, although we must recognize that he gives his own definition to his task.

It makes me a little embarrassed to hear "my theology" spoken of so seriously. Not, to be sure, because I think that what I am working at is something more or better than plain and honest theology. From the children's disease of being ashamed of theology, I think I have to some degree recovered . . .

I do not really come to you armed with a new and astonishing theology, but I want to take my place *among* you with a theology —which may also be your own—which consists simply in an understanding of and sympathy for the situation which every minister faces. Understand clearly therefore that I speak to you today more as a minister to colleagues than as a professor. The facts involved make this the only reasonable way to follow out your order. If then I have not only a *view*point, but something also of a *stand*point, it is simply the familiar standpoint of the man in the pulpit. Before him lies the Bible, full of mystery: and before him are seated his more or less numerous hearers, also full of mystery—

[5] In the original *Christian Dogmatics* (*Die Lehre vom Worte Gottes, Prolegomena zur christlichen Dogmatik,* Chr. Kaiser Verlag, München, 1927, p. ix). The above translation is from Paul Lehmann, "The Changing Course of a Corrective Theology," *Theology Today,* October 1956, p. 334.

and what indeed is more so? *What now?* asks the minister. If I could succeed in bringing acutely to your minds the whole content of that "what now?" I should have won you not only to my *stand*point, which indeed you occupy already, but also to my *view*point, no matter what you might think of my theology.[6]

Thus for Barth theology is the product of the reflection of both the preacher and the church about their proper message. It is the response that the church tries to give in every age to the decisive question of the content of preaching. A well-defined understanding of the church emerges here: it is not an institution, or a place for the conservation or the defense of moral and spiritual values, but a witnessing people, charged with responsibility for making the good news of the Kingdom of God heard in the world. Everything else must be subordinated to this proclamation, everything else must revolve around this message that is the church's very *raison d'être*. If the church corrupts this message, it corrupts itself. If it knows what to say at any step in world history, at that moment, it is truly the church, and becomes the church once again; it only *is* the church as it is *becoming* the church afresh each day. The task of theology, then, is constantly to recall and restore to the church its *raison d'être*, which is the content of its message.

In 1922 at Göttingen the journal *Zwischen den Zeiten* came into being, founded by Barth along with Thurneysen and Friedrich Gogarten. *Between the Times*—such a title is significant for the whole Barthian perspective. Between Pentecost and the coming of the Kingdom, in the time of "God's patience," which is itself the time of the Church, Christians are to ask themselves about the message of the church. "The Distress and Promise of Christian Preaching" (76) was the title of the article Barth wrote to inaugurate the journal. *Between the Times*—in retrospect the title has a political aspect as well, for it was the journal of the coming theological gener-

6 Barth, *The Word of God and the Word of Man*, Harper and Brothers (Torchbooks), New York, 1957, pp. 97, 103–4.

ation, asking itself about its responsibilities between the First and Second World Wars, in that strange interval in German history between the end of the German Empire and the rising tide of Hitlerism. The final issue of *Zwischen den Zeiten* appeared in the summer of 1933, at the moment when Hitler had attained unlimited power and seemed ready to make mincemeat of the German Evangelical Church.

THE DOGMATICS

In 1926 Barth left Göttingen to join the faculty at Münster in Westphalia, where he became the creative and independent theologian he has remained ever since. Up until this time, it appears, he had scarcely dared to try his own wings as a creator or innovator. With an extraordinary respect for the past, he devoted five semesters of lectures to establishing his foundations in the history of systematic theology. Calvin, Zwingli, Schleiermacher and the basic documents of Reformed theology (such as the Confession of Faith of La Rochelle and the Genevan Catechism) were the object of thorough and careful study, in which Barth took seriously the slightest nuances of the thought of the Reformation, which, from the sixteenth to the nineteenth century, he has succeeded in understanding better than anyone else in our time. It was only after this that he dared to offer an original course and to begin a dogmatic work of his own under the title "Instruction in the Christian Religion," the faculty having forbidden him to use the term "dogmatics," since at Göttingen the latter term was strictly reserved for Lutheran doctrine!

But at Münster, after he had published two commentaries, one on First Corinthians, giving particular attention to the climatic fifteenth chapter dealing with the resurrection,[7] and one on Philippians,[8] he launched out on his own, and in

[7] Barth, *The Resurrection of the Dead*, Fleming H. Revell Company, New York, 1933.
[8] Barth, *The Epistle to the Philippians*, John Knox Press, Richmond, Virginia, 1962.

1927 a new book emerged from the presses of the faithful Christian Kaiser Verlag of Münich, *The Doctrine of the Word of God, Prolegomena to a Christian Dogmatics* (116). This work, which several years later Barth disavowed, and which has never been translated, represents a kind of ingenious, unsuccessful experiment, the first sally of one whose powers are able to carry him farther than he had wished. It represents a preliminary sketch of the compendium of Christian learning that will later become the great *Church Dogmatics*—the huge work which in its turn will remain unfinished, for it is hard to see how a man in his seventies will have the strength and the time necessary to publish the five volumes that ought to be added to the twelve already completed, and thus bring to completion a work unequaled in the whole history of theology.[9]

It was not at Münster, however, but at Bonn, where he moved in 1930, that the *Church Dogmatics* began to be published in 1932. The title of this new work was carefully chosen, and corresponds perfectly to the stress, so decisive for Barth's thought, on theology as completely based on the message and life of the church. It was also while he was at Bonn that Barth wrote a little book entitled *Anselm: Fides Quaerens Intellectum*.[10] Without question this little study is one of the least well-known of his works, and yet, by his own admission, it is the book on which he "expended special care and devotion." In it he sets forth in a basic way the nature and method of theology. Jean Bosc comments on this as follows:

To seek to understand is part of what it means to have faith; not because comprehension or intelligence are necessary in order to come to faith or to affirm it, but because it is part of the very nature of faith itself to desire understanding. How could it be otherwise? The God in whom we believe is the truth, and his truth is ad-

[9] Translator's Note: Barth has already completed IV/4, and has hazarded the guess that Volume V can be completed in one volume, rather than many "part-volumes," since so much of the material it will contain has been anticipated in earlier portions of the work.
[10] Published by John Knox Press, Richmond, Virginia, 1960.

dressed to us as a truth which must as a result be known. To believe in him and as a result of that to love him, is to desire him and in so desiring him finally to choose truth and reject falsehood. To believe in him is finally to hope, that is, to await the day when in the glory of the Kingdom we shall see him face to face. To seek to understand is to take a step in the direction of this vision, and it is not only a step taken on the other side of faith, but a step of faith itself. In taking this step, the believer gives reasons to himself and to others for the faith which is in him, but he also enters into joy, for he discovers the beauty of the truth.

It is beyond question that all of this is an interpretation of the theological method of Anselm of Canterbury; but it is also clear that we must see in this commentary a setting forth of Barth's own intention: the rest of his work only serves to confirm this. Faith involves in its very nature this understanding by means of which the Christian gives a reason for his faith; and this understanding is truly a source of understanding and of joy.[11]

From this point on Barth is in full possession of his powers; he has found a place to stand, a word to speak and a way to work. He has many lively and receptive students, a whole generation of young pastors and laymen of all sorts who consider him the most formative influence on their thought. Among his colleagues in the German universities, Barth has many close friends and many real opponents. Churchmen begin to realize that something is really happening to challenge the conventionality of the church and shake the dust of the venerable ecclesiastical institutions. So Barth is watched, admired and feared.

1933!

Barth was prepared, both inwardly and outwardly, for his work, equipped from head to foot, when the events leading to Germany's overthrow demanded new things of him, and made him one of those exceptional individuals who shape history

[11] Jean Bosc, *Karl Barth*, Editions Berger-Levrault, Paris, 1957, pp. 7–8.

more than they are shaped by it. The whole German church struggle really ought to be retraced here, but since that is out of the question, we must outline the high points, in order to emphasize the decisive part taken by Barth in this confrontation in which it seemed that the Evangelical Church, divided, uncertain and tempted by nationalism, would be unable to withstand the brutal and insidious assault of Nazism.

What actually happened, however, was that the church stood erect again, regained the needed courage, patience and boldness, and approached its trial calmly, with something akin to the joy of the martyrs of the early church. Certainly all those who, along with Barth, believe that the church is not only a human institution but also the body of Christ, "the living community of the living Lord," affirm today that the transformation of the Evangelical Church in Germany before 1933 into the Confessing Church of 1934 could not have taken place apart from a miracle of the Holy Spirit. Barth had no plan of action; he simply let himself be led, step by step, by his reading of Scripture, by his theological inquiry, and by the church's prayers. But if the Holy Spirit was the author of the amazing spiritual resistance offered by a minority of German Protestants against the Hitler regime, Barth was (along with Martin Niemöller, Heinrich Vogel, Wilhelm Niesel and others) one of the providential instruments who, at this particular moment, were there to further God's purposes. Let us see what happened.

Roman Catholicism was suddenly sheltered from persecution by the compromising concordat of January 1934, a concordat signed by von Papen and Cardinal Pacelli, which foresaw the bishops' oath of fidelity to the regime and the prohibition of political activity by the priests. The Protestants, for their part, approached the ensuing struggle in disorderly fashion, without organic or spiritual unity. The Lutheran tradition of subjection to the established government, the nationalistic bent of the leaders of the church, the contempt in which the Weimar Republic had unanimously been held, all facilitated the Evangelical Church's willingness to be brought quickly into line as a tool of the Nazi party. The beginnings of the struggle were catastrophic. Those responsible for the "Evangelical Church of the German Nation," which was created on April 25, 1933, published an enthusiastic declaration:

A mighty National Movement has captured and exalted our German Nation. An all-embracing reorganization of the State is taking place within the awakened German people. We give our hearty assent to this turning-point of history. God has given us this: to Him be the glory.[12]

The movement of the "German Christians" based the doctrine of the new Evangelical Church on the key words of Nazism: "Nation, Race, *Führer.*"

We take our stand upon the ground of positive Christianity. We profess an affirmative and typical faith in Christ, corresponding to the German spirit of Luther and to a heroic piety . . .
We see in race, folk, and nation orders of existence granted and entrusted to us by God. God's law for us is that we look to the preservation of these orders . . .
In the mission to the Jews we perceive a grave danger to our nationality. It is an entrance gate for alien blood into our body politic. It has no justification for existence beside foreign missions. . . . In particular, marriage between Germans and Jews is to be forbidden.[13]

In the churches, flags with the swastika were unfurled, while the "Deutschland über alles" and the "Horst Wessels" song were sung alongside Luther's chorale "A Mighty Fortress is our God." In the church elections of July 1933, the candidates who were "German Christians," officially supported by Hitler, received more than seventy-five percent of the votes.

[12] Cited in Barth, *Theological Existence To-day!*, Hodder and Stoughton, London, 1933, p. 23.
[13] Cited in Cochrane, *The Church's Confession Under Hitler*, Westminster Press, Philadelphia, 1962, Appendix II, pp. 222–223.

THEOLOGISCHE EXISTENZ HEUTE

In the midst of this situation, early in July 1933, Barth and his friend Eduard Thurneysen launched a new theological journal, *Theologische Existenz heute,* the very name of which, *Theological Existence To-day!* sounded forth like the blast of a trumpet. The first issue, originally planned as a single tract, was an angry pamphlet, the most violent conceivable indictment of the "German Christians" and the official church. Seventeen thousand copies were sold in a single month. Here are some brief quotations from this manifesto, which was as decisive for the life of the church in the twentieth century as were Luther's Ninety-five Theses for the church of the sixteenth century:

As preachers and teachers of the Church, we are at one in fear but also in joy, that we are called to serve the Word of God within the Church and in the world by our preaching and our teaching. We agree, too, that with the fulfillment of our calling we not only see ourselves stand or fall, but we see everything that is important to us in this world, however precious or great it be, standing or falling. So that to us no concern can be more pressing, no hope more moving than the concern and hope of our ministry. No friend can be dearer than one who helps us in this ministry, no foe more hateful than he that wants to hinder us in this ministry. . . . On these things we agree or we are not preachers and teachers of the Church . . .[14]

Today we can lose our existence as theologians and teachers, which consists in our attachment to God's Word and plying our calling particularly to the ministry of the Word. . . . For the mighty temptation of this age, which appears in every shape possible, is that we no longer appreciate the intensity and exclusiveness of the demand which the Divine Word makes as such when looking at the force of other demands; so that in our anxiety in face of existing dangers we no longer put our whole trust in the authority

[14] *Theological Existence To-day!,* London, pp. 13–14.

of God's Word, but we think we ought to come to its aid with all sorts of contrivances, and we thus throw quite aside our confidence in the Word's power to triumph. . . . All this means that under the stormy assault of "principalities, powers, and rulers of this world's darkness," we seek for God elsewhere than in His Word, and seek His Word somewhere else than in Jesus Christ, and seek Jesus Christ elsewhere than in the Holy Scriptures of the Old and New Testaments. And so we become as those who do not seek for God at all . . .[15]

And therefore it is time to say, that under no circumstances should we, as theologians, forsake our theological existence and exchange our rights as "first-born" for "a mess of pottage." Or, said positively, that now, one and all, within the Church as she has borne us by means of the Word, and within the incomparable sphere of our vocation we must *abide,* or (if we have left it) *turn back* into the Church and into the sphere of our vocation, at all costs, by putting all regards and concerns behind . . .[16]

When it is recognized that [Jesus Christ] and *He alone* is the Leader, there is the possibility of theological existence. . . . Where there is no theological life about; when men *call out* for the Church leader instead of themselves *being* leaders in their appointed ministries; then all this crying out for a leader is as vain as the howling of the priests of Baal on Carmel, "Baal, hear us!"[17]

The resistance to Hitler had found its voice, its form and its leader. Henceforth nothing—not even prison or death—could stop the men, the church councils, or the parishes that were moved by such conviction.

Four other issues of *Theologische Existenz heute* were quickly published, and the journal became the place where the Confessing Church made its witness to the one true God, set forth its doctrine and received its nourishment. In two years, twenty-two issues came off the press and were widely distributed.

In 1934 the Confessing Church was formally organized. This was the period when there was no auditorium anywhere

15 *Ibid.,* p. 15.
16 *Ibid.,* p. 17.
17 *Ibid.,* p. 46.

in Germany big enough to hold those who came to hear Martin Niemöller speak. Even when he hired the Westphalia Hall in Dortmund, which has twenty-five thousand seats, he had to repeat his lecture in order to accommodate all those who could not find places to sit in the gigantic arena. This was also the period when the Confessing Church, in its synods and pastoral assemblies, defined the content of the Christian faith—polemically—in contrast to the heresy of the "German Christians" and the shocking racism that had become the official ideology of the new State.

More than ever Barth was the man of the hour, and his friendship with Niemöller became stronger and stronger. The Confessing Church was enlivened by this extraordinary pair, the one a Swiss democrat who was not a man of action but an intellectual in the best sense of the word, and the other a German nationalist, formerly the commanding officer of a submarine, a trouble maker by nature, and a man of intuition and action before anything else.

BARMEN

At Barmen, in Wuppertal, on May 31, 1934, a decisive document was drawn up which in subsequent church history will carry the name of the Barmen Confession, and will be included under this name in the collection of creedal affirmations by means of which the church, in every age, has proclaimed its faith when confronted by persecution and heresy. Barth was directly responsible for the text, having shaped the first draft of a confession of faith "in a few hours," according to Hans Asmussen, one of his companions at the time. (Barth jotted in the margin of one of the copies of Asmussen's article, ". . . while the others were taking their afternoon nap."[18])

[18] Cf. Hans Asmussen, "Karl Barth and the Confessing Church," in *Die Freiheit der Gebunden*, a *Festschrift* presented to Barth on his fiftieth birthday, in Munich, May 10, 1936.

Here are the opening paragraphs of the Barmen Confession:

In view of the errors of the "German Christians" of the present Reich Church government which are devastating the Church and are also thereby breaking up the unity of the German Evangelical Church, we confess the following evangelical truths:

1. "I am the way, and the truth, and the life; no one comes to the Father, but by me." (John 14:6) "Truly, truly, I say to you, he who does not enter the sheepfold by the door but climbs in by another way, that man is a thief and a robber. . . . I am the door; if anyone enters by me, he will be saved." (John 10:1, 9)

Jesus Christ, as he is attested for us in Holy Scripture, is the one Word of God which we have to hear and which we have to trust and obey in life and in death.

We reject the false doctrine, as though the Church could and would have to acknowledge as a source of its proclamation, apart from and beside this one Word of God, still other events and powers, figures and truths, as God's revelation.[19]

The other five articles of the Confession spell out what this means.

The second article stresses the fact that the whole life of the Christian belongs under the Lordship of Christ, and repudiates any kind of spiritual dichotomy or false separation between the sacred and the secular.

The third article stresses the freedom of the church—under orders from its one Lord—against the demands and political systems of this world.

The fourth article emphasizes the universal priesthood, the basic equality of all Christians before God, and repudiates the *"Führer-*principle" of special leaders as applied to the church.

The fifth article emphasizes the sovereignty of the Word of God over the laws of the state.

The sixth article stresses the Church's responsibility with

---

[19] Cited in Cochrane, *op. cit.*, Appendix VII, p. 239. A short account of Barth's interpretation of the events of Barmen can be found in *Church Dogmatics*, II/1, pp. 172–178.

respect to all people, and the independence of its message from all ideology or propaganda.

The confession concludes with an invitation addressed to all Christians in Germany to unite with the Confessing Church.

CONTINUED WITNESS TO THE FAITH

With the Barmen Confession it seemed that Barth had done the most important thing for the Confessing Church that he could do from within. He remained for some time at Bonn, where in 1935 he published *Credo*,[20] a series of lectures on the Apostles' Creed. But in the spring of this same year he was forced out of Germany by the Nazis, and after having vainly waited for an invitation to settle in France, he returned to his native city of Basel, which, being right on the German border, was ideally situated for observing and urging on the struggle from which the decree of expulsion had been designed to remove him. In Basel Barth kept in touch with what was going on elsewhere in the church, for he was constantly receiving information and welcoming men who succeeded in crossing the border, and he was proudly and secretly educating students who had been refused admission to the German universities.

Now less directly involved in action, and having more time, Barth wrote constantly, and published pamphlets, articles for religious and secular journals, lectures and sermons, in all of which he confronted the whole world with the basic reasons for spiritual resistance to Nazism. Exiled to his native land, and often under suspicion by his own government, Barth's vigor, clarity, involvement and authority were at least as significant now as his very presence had been in Bonn. The following excerpt from a speech at Basel in 1937 will show how this was so:

[20] Published by Charles Scribner's Sons (The Scribner Library), New York, 1962.

Let me begin with a little anecdote about something that happened at Darmstadt. A conference organized by the church was about to be held. The Gestapo intervened and tried to forbid the meeting, just as has happened countless times in Germany in the last few years. There was some bargaining between the leaders of the Gestapo and organizers of the conference. At the height of the discussion the police officer said to the pastors, "Gentlemen, it has come to the point where *you must decide whom you are going to obey. Will you obey me, the visible representative of the State, or this imaginary Lord you are always prattling about?*" Those were his words—an "imaginary Lord," therefore invisible, fabricated, unreal. I don't need to tell you who he was describing with these words. This one outburst of the Nazi official explains the whole German church struggle . . .

Do you expect here in Switzerland that the church (for we also have a church in our midst) should do the same thing *right now* that the German Confessing Church has done in its struggle? If you answer me, "No, we don't expect to do this," then I must ask you another question, "Why don't you expect to?" I imagine there is no one here who wants to make unfair charges against the church. It would be kinder to state that the church lacks neither zeal, nor ardor, nor concern about the examination of the problems of the times, and that it truly participates in the needs of national life. But perhaps its shortcomings are to be found elsewhere. Our church, our very own church, still believes far too much in a good man and far too little in the only good Master. Too much and too little—that is why our church is perhaps no longer the light that lightens the darkness, which is what the church ought to be. It is a much too feeble church, a liberal church, just like the German church that was overthrown in 1933.

And, because I am here to talk about the church, I am eager in conclusion to ask one more question: Who therefore *is* the church, the church right here as well as elsewhere? There's an easy answer to the question: the church is the pastors or at least the pious folk. No, *the church is composed of all those who, in some way or other, hear the call of the "imaginary Lord."* If I have succeeded in making clear to you that this call is also addressed to *us*, to anybody in our midst, then this speech will not have been in vain.[21]

---

[21] Cited in *Foi et vie*, No. 93–94, pp. 301f.

THE LETTERS TO THE CHURCHES

In the midst of all this activity, the second "part-volume" of the *Church Dogmatics* appeared in 1938—over a thousand pages in length! Meanwhile Barth was involved in widespread correspondence with all the countries that, near or far, immediately or in the long run, were threatened by Nazism. Before the crisis of September 1938 and the Munich conference, Barth wrote to the Czechs, through Professor Joseph Hromadka, urging them to resist. Then in September 1939 and October 1940 he warned and encouraged the French Protestants. A similar letter was written to the English in 1941, to the Norwegians in April 1942, to the Dutch in July, and to the Americans in October, of the same year. All these letters with their wisdom and clear prophetic quality were collected in one volume and published in 1945 as *A Swiss Voice* (310).[22]

Through these letters Barth gained considerable stature. He emerged as a trusted guide whose right judgments were sought by everyone as a way of understanding what was needed in order to see the situation clearly, to resist and simply to go on living. There is not a trace of fanaticism in these letters, which are full of good sense and down to earth realism. Occasionally there is a touch of humor, followed by a statement of faith so serene and yet so strong that it almost seems tangible.

Another dominant characteristic of these letters is the tone in which they are written. There is not a trace of stern judgment, and sarcasm seldom enters in. The dominant note is

[22] Translator's Note: The following portions of *Eine Schweizer Stimme* are available in English: "Church and State," in *Community, State, and Church*, Doubleday and Company (Anchor Books), Garden City, New York, 1960; *The Church and the Political Problem of Our Day*, Charles Scribner's Sons, New York, 1939; *This Christian Cause*, The Macmillan Company, New York, 1941; *The Church and the War*, The Macmillan Company, New York, 1944; *The Only Way* (including "Can the Germans Be Cured?" and "The Germans and Ourselves"), Philosophical Library, New York, 1947.

tenderness: in the name of love of Christ, the conqueror of death, a father writes to his children; he encourages them, consoles them and calls them to courageousness, patience, clearheadedness and martyrdom if need be. And behind every statement, as the focal point for every comment, hovers the message of the Kingdom of God, where the love of God who has conquered death will triumph forever.

It is not surprising that these letters should be read and re-read everywhere, or that they should be circulated secretly as clandestine literature, or that "Barthian" prose should be considered by the totalitarian police as one of the worst kinds of anti-Nazi literature. During this time both Barth, at liberty in Switzerland, and Niemöller, in a concentration camp, were regarded as the two most dangerous public enemies of the Nazi regime.

SPOKESMAN FOR THE DEFEATED GERMANS

But in 1945, when the glow of liberation extended clear across Europe, Barth published two small pamphlets, "The Germans and Ourselves," and "Can The Germans Be Cured?"[23] With an audacity based on love he wrote:

The condition *sine qua non* for the German cure is that the German people, whether under their own sovereignty or otherwise, be given political freedom: that is, the possibility of learning to be responsible for their own thinking and acting. . . . The Allies should impose this task upon the Germans as soon as possible.[24]

What does this sort of talk mean? How can it be that the man who wrote as he did to Hromadka back in 1938 can write this way in 1945?

Here we observe the distance that separates the partisan from the prophet. Barth expressed himself as he did during

[23] Translator's Note: Published in English as one volume, *The Only Way.*
[24] "Can the Germans Be Cured?" in *op. cit.*, p. 8.

the whole Hitlerian epoch not because he was a Swiss democrat, but because he was a theologian of the sole sovereignty
of God. Toward the one invisible Lord whom Barth wished to
proclaim in all that he did, the Nazi idolatry represented a
kind of defiance that could not be ignored. To the victims of
Hitler's Reich, as well as to Hitler's accomplices, Barth had to
keep pounding home for a dozen years that God is not
mocked, and that his judgment will not spare a regime in
which anti-Semitism clearly demonstrates how radically anti-
Christian it is.

Then came the collapse of Germany and her allies in a
defeat more complete and bloody than could have been imag-
ined, which Barth and the whole Confessing Church could
only view, in fear and trembling, as a fulfillment of what they
had declared, and as a contemporary example of the preaching
of the Old Testament prophets about the fall of Babylon.

And it was at that time, during the obliteration bombing
of the German cities, during the destruction of all her political and social structures, during the dismemberment of Germany into four occupation zones, during a time when no one
was speaking in the name of the German people or the German church, that Barth once again spoke the word that
needed to be spoken. It was a word that Roosevelt and
Churchill had known enough to speak during the darkest
hours of the war, but which, in the joy of victory and in the
horror of the discovery of what had gone on in the concentration camps, the victors were only too willing to forget—namely
that it was not against the German people, but only against
the Hitlerian regime, that this battle had been waged. Now
that the victory was won, it was vitally important not to destroy those who, while they had surely been Hitler's accomplices, had also been his first victims, namely the Germans
themselves. In the Allies' hour of triumph and liberation, the
future of Germany ought to be one of their major concerns.

A partisan cannot speak this way. Only a prophet can—if we
understand the word in its Old Testament sense, not so much
a man who predicts the future, but a man who, in every

epoch, is concerned that his contemporaries hear the Word of the sovereign God. Such a word is never heard in nationalistic propaganda and slogans, it never follows the crowd and never rejoices in the death of the sinner. Rather, in every kind of situation this word opens up a more than human perspective, a vertical perspective toward the God who secretly controls the destiny of men and the history of nations. For the sovereign God who opposes the violent is also the God whose grace raises up and offers a new beginning to those who were destroyed by his judgment.

And this is why Barth insisted that the question for 1945 was the question, "How can the Germans be cured?" This apparent reversal conceals a deep and compelling logic, founded on and justified by the central dialectic of the absolute sovereignty of God, whose glory and good pleasure consist always in saving his enemies, and whose judgment is never negative and destructive, but always a source of life, a way into the future and a starting point toward a new world.

In these two pamphlets Barth became the spokesman for the defeated Germans, with an appealing earnestness that excluded neither clearheadedness nor realism.

In war and in peace, there have always and everywhere been lies and slavery, brutality and great outbreaks of such inhumanity as cries to heaven. We must certainly not forget that our own ancestors, who for the rest, and with right, are highly extolled, were, in their very time of martial splendour, not in the least angelic. But the Germany of today—and this distinguishes it also from revolutionary Russia, has raised inhumanity to a principle, a system and a method. National Socialism is not only bound up but also identical with inhumanity. All theoretical objections of this order which were formerly raised against its thoughts and teachings have been far surpassed by its practice; for meantime by its practice it has with an ever increasing clarity shown its true nature and (one may assuredly add) condemned itself.[25]

[25] "The Germans and Ourselves," in *op. cit.*, pp. 69–70.

We should like to know, and we ought to know, if what the present spokesmen of the German people, who are at the same time its bitterest enemies, assert is really true—namely, that the overwhelming majority of this people has desired and explicitly and tacitly approved and in its heart is in sympathy with what has been done for twelve years in its name. Alternatively, we should like to know, and we ought to know, if the reverse is true, as the "Free Germany" of General Von Seydlitz from Moscow, or wherever it may be, assures us—namely, that the overwhelming majority of this people is itself but the first and most lamentable victim of version? Or is a third version correct, which claims that the German actions which dominate the picture today. Which is the correct version? Or is a third version correct, which claims that the German is in a quite peculiar way a being with two completely different mentalities, so that in every German one would have to look simultaneously for something of Friedrich Schiller and Matthias Claudius as well as something of Joseph Goebbels and Heinrich Himmler, something of the spirit of Weimar as well as the spirit of Potsdam? But over and above all that, there seems to be something like a spirit—represented by not a few Germans—of Oradour and Oswiecim.[26]

There is a text in the Old Testament in which may be recognized almost word for word what is now happening and will happen in Germany. It is in the fourteenth chapter of the prophet Isaiah, where there is a song about the fall of the King of Babylon, whose most vigorous passage contains the famous words:

How art thou fallen from heaven, O Lucifer, son of the morning!
How art thou cut down to the ground, which didst weaken the nations!
For thou has said in thine heart, I will ascend unto heaven, I will exalt my throne above the stars of God:
I will set also upon the mount of the congregation, in the sides of the North:

[26] *Ibid.*, pp. 72–73. Oradour was a French village that was destroyed, and the inhabitants shot or burned, on June 10, 1944. Oswiecim was a concentration camp in Poland.

I will ascend above the heights of the clouds;
I will be like the most High.
Yet thou shalt be brought down to hell, to the sides of the pit.

A song of triumph? So it is called, unfortunately, in German
editions. Yes; it certainly does not show pity, it certainly shows
triumph, but the triumph is veiled by something quite different,
by a deep sympathy with what is described, by a deep awe which
at the same time helps him who has been stricken down, who from
such a height has fallen so low.

This is how we should look at the Germans when they appear
before us again—deeply moved, with sympathy, with awe. We
should look at them like this, even when we cannot help agreeing
that things were in justice bound to end this way, even when we
cannot wish that this war might have had a different conclusion.
We should judge ourselves if now, when everything is happening
before our very eyes as it was bound to happen, we were able to
avoid this deep emotion and sympathy and awe.[27]

How can the Germans be cured? . . . The German cure de-
pends wholly—and so does the cure of all Europe—on choosing,
out of the various human conceptions—and I refer to the Allies
as well as to the Germans—the one I would like to mention in my
conclusion: Christian Realism.[28]

What is important now is neither the settling up of ac-
counts nor mutual and contradictory self-justification. The essential thing in 1945 is that all together should begin to recon-
struct a world fashioned for man, which would be fully open
to charity, justice and progress. Whatever stands in the way of
this kind of future, however important it might seem by itself,
ought to be thrust aside. Negative activity must be disavowed.
The task of true reconstruction is the common task to which
all men of good will are bid, whether they are Christians or
not.

It is not surprising that statements of this sort made quite
an impact. The characteristic of the prophetic word is that it
is always unexpected and therefore always disturbing, and

[27] *Ibid.*, pp. 87–88.
[28] "Can the Germans be Cured?" in *op. cit.*, pp. 16–17.

there was no unanimity of response to Barth's appeal. Ranged against him were all the superpatriots, the western and particularly the French nationalists who wanted to destroy Germany forever, the Soviet nationalists who favored the disappearance of Germany as an independent and united state, and the German nationalists for whom the defeat had been an accident for which the now conquered Hitler was solely to blame. On the other hand, men from many countries, strongly represented by those who were released from concentration camps, hailed Barth's words as sensible, reasonable and positive. But, sad to relate, international politics failed to take into account that Germany's conquerors had a responsibility for Germany's future as great as the capitulation they had just imposed on that country. They promptly began treating conquered Germany as a pawn, availing themselves of Germany's partition as a weapon, of its natural resources and industrial potential as arsenals, and of its men as cheap labor. Those whom Barth had called to Germany's bedside as doctors to heal her were concerned only for themselves; in restoring the prosperity of the two Germanies, as was done in various ways, they put their own concerns first.

As a result, fifteen years after the victory over Hitler's Reich, the German question is still an open wound in the side of world peace. As a result of neither having known how nor having wished to cure conquered Germany, yesterday's conquerors have endangered international peace to an alarming degree. The Berlin question is the most critical instance of this, but it is far from being the only one.

On the other hand, those within the Confessing Church received Barth's message with immense gratitude, and we can assert that it lies behind one of the most important declarations in the history of Christendom. On October 18–19, 1945, when the Council of the Evangelical Church in Germany and the federation of the *Landeskirchen* in Germany were reunited for the first time, a delegation from the World Council of Churches came to Stuttgart to meet the Germans, now that the war was over. After a long and moving discussion, the Germans, under Niemöller's inspiration, drew up a statement now known as the Stuttgart Declaration, a statement dealing with the guilt of the German nation and the church. The key phrase of the declaration reads: "We are not only conscious of oneness with our nation in a great community of suffering, but also in a solidarity of guilt."[29]

Such an attitude was a clear indication of healing, and it offered a genuine basis for continued encounter in peace and mutual confidence. It assured the return of German Protestantism into the ecumenical community and did much to strengthen the conviction that Christians in postwar Germany had really learned the lessons of the Hitlerian torment.

As early as 1945, Barth went back to Germany. One can imagine the emotion with which the man of Barmen, the spokesman for spiritual resistance to Nazism, met again with the friends of whom he had never stopped thinking, and for whom he had never stopped fighting, during his apparent retreat in Basel. One thing Barth clearly demonstrated during these years was the way in which even the most systematic kind of theology involves one in the world, and the way in which intercession keeps one close to others. Without any difficult or apparent problem, Barth met with those with whom he had been a close companion in spite of the frontier —particularly Niemöller, about whom he wrote a penetrating article in 1945. Niemöller, scarcely released from eight years in a concentration camp, took a clear stand on all issues with admirable and enviable freedom. The friendship between these two very different men deepened in proportion to their complete forthrightness with one another. During one of their meetings, which were always difficult and yet productive, Barth said to Niemöller, "You haven't the least idea what theology is all about, and yet how can I complain? For you think and see and do the right things!" To which Niemöller replied, "You can't stop thinking theologically for a moment,

29 Cited in Franklin Littell, *The German Phoenix*, Doubleday and Company, Garden City, New York, 1960, p. 189.

and yet how can I complain? For you think and see and do the right things too!"

In all kinds of articles, interviews and lectures, Barth continued to interpret Germany and the idea of spiritual resistance to the rest of the world, and to put things in proper perspective. With clarity and precision he continued to trace the course that must be followed, as he saw it in the light of Scripture, in order to avoid the repetition of disastrous errors.

In 1946, after several brief trips, Barth accepted an invitation to return to Bonn for a semester of regular teaching, and found himself in the ruins of his old university teaching dogmatics, a discipline more than ever necessary for a generation of young postwar theologians who were confused by the nihilistic revolution and the Russian winters they had endured. Many empty places were apparent in the ranks of his former listeners; the best of them had been systematically exposed to danger or, like Dietrich Bonhoeffer, executed in concentration camps.

In 1947 he returned to Bonn for another semester. After he had completed these semesters at Bonn—almost as though he had needed to display the visible revenge of the theologian over the dictator!—Barth published a small volume called *Dogmatics in Outline*,[30] written in a vigorous and concise style, full of theological insight and crammed with references to the present and the immediate past. Once again he returned to the Apostles' Creed and interpreted it with vigor, depth and simplicity. All the experience and labor of forty years of theological study were placed at the service of the younger generation, who were both excited and disconcerted to discover in this ageing man, speaking German with an impossible Swiss accent, the most youthful, most obstreperous, most exacting and exciting teacher they had ever known.

But contemporary Germany not only includes the federal republic with its ruins, which the western interests were soon to restore in spectacular fashion; it also includes East Ger-

[30] Published by Harper and Brothers (Torchbooks), New York, 1959.

many, an integral part of the Soviet-dominated portion of Europe. Several times Barth went to Berlin—in 1946 he even went to Dresden—where he met with Russian occupation authorities and German communists, as well as with representatives of the church in East Germany, which was soon to be put to the test in most urgent fashion. The Russian authorities and the German communists, who were all set to make a great to-do over the "anti-Fascist" Barth, soon discovered that he was not their man and that they had been deceived if they counted on him to carry water for the mill of eastern propaganda.

BARTH AND COMMUNISM

In the spring of 1948 Barth took a trip to Hungary, in the course of which he was able to ascertain the degree of vitality of the Reformed Church in Hungary, which was under a communist regime that was already one of the strictest in eastern Europe.[31]

Here we must come to terms with a difficult matter. On various sides, Barth is attacked for not having taken as radically negative an attitude toward communism as he did toward Nazism. However, if one reads the letter Barth sent to Secretary of State Zaisser on March 2, 1953, concerning the arrest of pastors in East Germany,[32] or the more recent "Letter to a Pastor in the German Democratic Republic,"[33] it is clear that he is not guilty of complacency or partiality toward Marxism. However that may be, it is also clear that Barth is no longer—as he was from 1933 to 1945—the untiring sentinel

[31] Translator's Note: A number of documents by Barth relative to this trip are collected in *Against the Stream*, S. C. M. Press, London, 1954.
[32] This letter was written at the time of a persecution that caused great havoc between February and July, 1953, in East Germany. During it a great many pastors were arrested and sentenced to long prison terms, before being pardoned in the middle of July. See *Antwort* bibliography, 384.
[33] Available in English in Barth-Hamel, *How to Serve God in a Marxist Land*, Association Press, New York, 1959.

warning the world of the dangers and threats of dictatorship. Why has he chosen to be relatively silent today? When pressed on this, Barth replies:

1. When Hitler took power in 1933, he did so with the consent and complicity of the whole world. Not only the Germans, but the western democracies, the Russians and even the Swiss, tolerated, accepted and approved the establishment of his dictatorship. By a series of successive blunders or acts of cowardice, of which the best known are the Munich Agreement and the German-Soviet Pact, the rest of the world played along with the game of nationalism and contributed to its entrenchment in power. Within the church, those who denounced the idolatrous character of anti-Semitic nationalism were a tiny minority. It was important then not only to strengthen the spiritual resistance, but to assume leadership, no matter what happened. Then one was inevitably alone and apparently defeated, and it was necessary to swim against the stream and accept whatever risks came with doing so.

Today, however, the western world is lined up against the USSR, displaying an attitude of fear and aggressiveness. Anti-communism is the dominant attitude found in the political and religious press, and it is one of the recurring themes in the church's preaching and teaching. There is no danger of ideological contamination: the left-wing partisans of peace, in West Germany and elsewhere, have won only a tiny minority of Christians to their cause, and all the rest are constantly showing how wrong they are. When anti-communism has official spokesmen even within the Evangelical Church, from extremists like Hans Asmussen to moderates like Helmut Gollwitzer, there is no need to add another voice to the chorus. Furthermore, it is important not to react against communist totalitarianism and its demonic endeavors simply in the name of indiscriminate anti-communism. It is another thing, and much more important, to resist communism in the name of the sovereignty of the God of the gospel.

2. It is important to remember that western anti-commu-

nism can be a danger to the West itself. To the degree that the free world finds its meaning only in preparation for a future war or in actual tests of force against the eastern bloc, it jeopardizes its own *raison d'être*, for nationalism, militarism, social conservatism and the power of international capitalism are the reverse side of the coin of anti-communism. All these represent temptations for western man that are indeed subtle, but that in the long run appear more destructive than do the temptations of communism for eastern man. At any rate, to the degree that the church is blindly and uncritically identified with the ideology and materialism of western culture (an identification particularly dangerous when it is not recognized as such), it is in danger of losing its own *raison d'être* and the authenticity of its message. It is in greater danger, in fact, than it is when confronted by the outrage of overt persecution or the covert hostility that it must endure on the other side of the Iron Curtain.

3. Communism can never be defeated solely by anti-communist propaganda and military strength. Only if the West works out a positive social order, guaranteeing the freedoms essential for individual and social justice, will it have responded truly to the challenge of communist ideology and strategy. In this respect, the colonial wars of the West are the highest trump cards in the communist deck.

4. The constant threat of force against communism, the brinkmanship practiced by the West, following in the footsteps of John Foster Dulles and various theologians and theorists of all sorts, is dangerous to the extreme. If pressed too far it will lead to World War III, the catastrophic nature of which cannot be doubted in the atomic age, even if it does not destroy everybody. It is not in this fashion, therefore, that the church ought to act. Both in the East and in the West the church owes it to itself, and owes it to its Lord, to stand between East and West and untiringly to build bridges, establish connecting links and outline steps toward reconciliation, by means of which peace can be established.

Agreeing once more with Niemöller, Barth therefore asks Christians living under communist rule to be quite clear about the nature of the State in which they are living, but also and above all not to cease believing that *there also* the living God is sovereign, and that *there also* it is important to be humbly faithful in whatever situation the Lord of the church has placed us. Beyond that, Barth remains silent. Not only the word of the prophet, but also his silence, can be disturbing and significant.

Nevertheless, early in 1960, when *The Christian Century* asked Barth to comment on the preceding decade, he responded in clear-cut fashion in an article which unfortunately cannot be quoted in full. He began by explaining with his unquenchable humor—that humor without which he cannot be understood and which he ranks near the top of the Christian virtues—that a new science, gerontology, has come into being at a most opportune time, since he now represents its concern. The object of this young branch of medicine is what can be done for a man who is growing old. So be it! Even his "work pace at the desk," he writes, "is becoming slower." His children and grandchildren are spread from Chicago to Djakarta, the *Dogmatics* is still not finished—and the world is still the world.

The East-West question has accompanied and shadowed us all since the end of World War II. On this question I cannot agree with the great majority of those around me. Not that I have any inclination toward Eastern communism, in view of the face it presents to the world. I decidedly prefer not to live within its sphere and do not wish anyone else to be forced to do so. But I do not comprehend how either politics or Christianity require or even permit such a disinclination to lead to the conclusions which the West has drawn with increasing sharpness in the past fifteen years. I regard anti-Communism as a matter of principle an evil even greater than Communism itself. Can one overlook the fact that Communism is the unwelcomed yet—in all its belligerence —natural result of Western developments? Has not its total, inhuman compulsion, of which we complain so much, haunted our avowedly free Western society in another form from remotest times? And was it then something suddenly new and worthy of special horror when Communism presented itself as a doctrine of salvation blessing all men and nations and therefore one to be spread over the whole world? Are there not other systems of this kind and tendency? Further, could we really intend to help the peoples governed by Communism and the world threatened by it, or even one individual among those suffering under its effects, by proclaiming and seeking to practice toward it a relationship exclusively that of enemies? Have we forgotten that what is at stake in this "absolute enemy" relationship, to which every brave man in the West is now obligated and for which he would give his all, is a typical invention of (and a heritage from) our defunct dictators—and that only the "Hitler in us" can be an anti-Communist on principle? . . .

What kind of Western philosophy and political ethics—and unfortunately even theology—was it whose wisdom consisted of recasting the Eastern collective man into an angel of darkness and the Western "organization man" into an angel of light? And then with the help of such metaphysics and mythology (the fact of an Eastern counterpart is no excuse!) bestowing on the absurd "cold war" struggle its needed higher consecration? Were we so unsure of the goodness of the Western cause and of the power of resistance of Western man that we could bring ourselves to admit only senselessly unequal alternatives—freedom and the dignity of man as against mutual atomic annihilation—then venture to pass off just this latter alternative as a work of true Christian love? . . .

I think above all that the Christian churches should have considered it their commission to influence by superior witness to the peace and hope of the kingdom of God both public opinion and the leaders who are politically responsible. The churches have injured the cause of the gospel by the manner, to a great extent thoughtless, in which they have identified the gospel (in this case Rome is no better than Geneva and Geneva no better than Rome!) with the badly planned and ineptly guided cause of the West. The cause of the gospel cannot from the human perspective be healed for a long time by even the best ecumenical and missionary efforts. The churches have provided Eastern godlessness with new arguments difficult to overcome instead of refuting it by practical action.[34]

THE ATOMIC BOMB

Barth can always break his silence when he deems it necessary. As a result he has been actively involved in the struggle against atomic war carried on in most countries for the last few years. In company with Niemöller, and once again disagreeing with the church, he believes that the mounting armaments race, pursued to the point where humanity now has the effective means of destroying itself, is a demonic and suicidal undertaking. Public opinion everywhere must be mobilized to halt this tendency before it is too late. Evidence of Barth's concern is found in the following comments he sent to the European Congress for Outlawing Atomic Weapons, which met in London in 1959:

1. From every quarter during the last few years, conclusive arguments showing the evil and the danger of atomic weapons have been advanced with all possible clarity and have been brought to everyone's attention. He who has ears to hear let him hear.
2. We find ourselves confronted, however, by a threefold fact:
a. Our governments see the problem clearly, and they recognize or at least do not deny its gravity, but they have decided all the same to pursue and carry our their fatal course of action.
b. Although for the most part our people are—secretly but in part openly also—deeply frightened by the terrible threat of atomic weapons, they are not ready to advocate opposition or even clear-cut resistance on the matter.
c. The intelligentsia in particular, along with a large group of the church leaders, willingly devote themselves to profound philosophical and theological discussions about such problems as the

[34] "Recapitulation Number Three," in *The Christian Century*, January 20, 1960, pp. 72–73; also available in Harold Fey, ed., *How My Mind Has Changed*, Meridian Books, 1961, pp. 27–31.

tragic dimension of man's existence in the atomic age, but they stubbornly avoid making any specific decision against atomic weapons.

3. The reason for this inner contradiction is found in the fear of a supposedly greater threat aimed by the enemy at all that is most sacred, which confronts us both ideologically and politically. This threat, it is held, can be forestalled only by recourse to the counter-threat of atomic weapons.

4. Unless we succeed in destroying this ideological and political opposition, along with the mutual anxiety which follows in its wake, we will not be able to overcome the contradiction that exists between the good ideas and evil practices of our governments, the majority of our people, our leaders, and those within our churches. And if this contradiction cannot be overcome, we will have to reckon with the blasphemous and deadly development of atomic weapons.

5. Therefore the basic task of those who oppose atomic weapons ought to consist in a new effort, free from all prejudice, to overcome this ideological and political opposition. In other words, the opponents of atomic weapons must adopt and exemplify a position that is not only exempt from this mutual anxiety, but is also based uniquely on God and a true understanding of man.

6. It goes without saying that opposition to atomic weapons must continue on all levels everywhere, and in every situation as circumstances may require, quite independently of this larger context, and consequently without taking into consideration the matter of immediate success or defeat.

7. A final question is raised, and it is possible that the Congress ought to take a stand on it—namely that of deciding, since the matter has now been sufficiently discussed, whether this opposition ought not to be made specific by means of active resistance, perhaps in the form of an open invitation to refuse to serve in military units employing such weapons.

Karl Barth,
Basel,
January 7, 1959

CHRISTIANS AND PUBLIC LIFE

During the postwar years Barth completed and published a number of important articles, including many that dealt with Christian political responsibility. Although occupied with the matter for many years, he now clarified and developed his thought with greater precision. Set forth in an important lecture on *Church and State* given in 1938, Barth's position has received its fullest expression in a little study on *The Christian Community and the Civil Community*, published in 1946, which is one of the high points of contemporary theology.[35] It is impossible to summarize it here, for every word is weighted with its own meaning and significance. In the universal Lordship of Christ over the Church and the State, Barth sees the decisive and indisputable foundation of a political responsibility that Christians cannot avoid. The following excerpts present the gist of his argument:

The Christian community is particularly conscious of the need for the existence of the civil community. For it knows that all men (non-Christians as well as Christians) need to have "kings," that is, need to be subject to an external, relative and provisional order of law, defended by superior authority and force. It knows that the original and final pattern of this order is the eternal Kingdom of God and the eternal righteousness of His grace. It preaches the Kingdom of God in this eternal form. But it also thanks God that His Kingdom has an external, relative and provisional embodiment (in the world that is not yet redeemed) in which it is valid and effective even when the temporal order is based on the most imperfect and clouded knowledge of Jesus Christ or on no such knowledge at all. This external, relative and provisional, but not

[35] Translator's Note: Both essays are available in *Community, State, and Church*, pp. 101–148, and 149–189, respectively. "The Christian Community and the Civil Community" is also available in *Against the Stream*, pp. 15–50. On the whole problem see the illuminating essay by Will Herberg, "The Social Philosophy of Karl Barth," introducing *Community, State, and Church*, pp. 11–67.

on that account invalid or ineffective, form of legal order is the civil community. The Christian community is aware of the need for the civil community, and it alone takes the need absolutely seriously. For—because it knows of the Kingdom and grace of God —it knows of man's presumption and the plainly destructive consequences of man's presumption. It knows how dangerous man is and how endangered by himself. It knows him as a sinner, that is as a being who is always on the point of opening the sluices through which, if he were not checked in time, chaos and nothingness would break in and bring human time to an end. It can only conceive the time that is still left to it as a "time of grace" in the twofold sense of being the time which it is given in order to know and lay hold of God's grace—and as the time which it is given for this very purpose by the grace of God. The Christian community itself exists in this time which is given to man, that is, in the space where man's temporal life is still protected from chaos—and on the face of it chaos should have broken in long ago. It sees as the visible means of this protection of human life from chaos the existence of the civil community, the State's effort to achieve an external, relative and provisional humanising of man's life and the political order instituted for all (for non-Christians as well as Christians—they both need it, for human arrogance is alive in both), under which the evil are punished and the good rewarded (Rom. 13:3, 1 Pet. 2:14) and which guarantees that the worst is prevented from happening. It knows that without this political order there would be no Christian order. It knows and it thanks God that—as the inner circle within the wider circle (cf. O. Cullmann, *Königsherrschaft Christi und Kirche im Neuen Testament*, 1941)—it is allowed to share the protection which the civil community affords.[36]

The State can assume the face and character of Pilate. Even then, however, it still acts in the power which God has given it ("Thou couldest have no power at all against me, except it were given thee from above," John 19:11). Even in its perversion it cannot escape from God; and His law is the standard by which it is judged. The Christian community therefore acknowledges "the benefaction of this ordinance of His with thankful, reverent hearts"

[36] The Christian Community and the Civil Community," in *Against the Storm*, pp. 19–20.

(Barmen Thesis No. 5). The benefaction which it acknowledges consists in the external, relative and provisional sanctification of the unhallowed world which is brought about by the existence of political power and order. In what concrete attitudes to political patterns and realities this Christian acknowledgement will be expressed can remain a completely open question. It makes one thing quite impossible, however: a Christian decision to be indifferent; a non-political Christianity. The Church can in no case be indifferent or neutral towards this manifestation of an order so clearly related to its own mission.[37]

Only an act of supreme disobedience on the part of Christians could bring the special existence of the Christian community to an end. Such a cessation is also impossible because then the voice of what is ultimately the only hope and help which all men need to hear would be silent.[38]

THE HUMANITY OF GOD

In addition to his political writing, Barth has also examined the development of his own thought. Shortly after his seventieth birthday, which was celebrated with joy and thankfulness by his friends in the theological world, Barth wrote the following in a lecture given at Aarau on September 25, 1956, on "The Humanity of God":

Permit me to give my exposition of this theme first in the form of a report. In a consideration of the earlier change referred to above, a viewpoint regarding the urgent new task of the succeeding period and of today will emerge.[39]

Evangelical theology almost all along the line, certainly in all its representative forms and tendencies, had become *religionistic, anthropocentric,* and in this sense *humanistic.* . . . There is no question about it: here man was made great at the cost of God.[40]

---

[37] *Ibid.,* p. 22.
[38] *Ibid.,* p. 23.
[39] Barth, *The Humanity of God,* John Knox Press, Richmond, Virginia, 1960, p. 38.
[40] *Ibid.,* p. 39.

Or was it something more fundamental than all that, namely, the discovery that the theme of the Bible, contrary to the critical and to the orthodox exegesis which we inherited, certainly could not be man's religion and religious morality and certainly not his own secret divinity?[41]

All this, however well it may have been meant and however much it may have mattered, was nevertheless said somewhat severely and brutally, and moreover—at least according to the other side—in part heretically. How we cleared things away! And we did almost nothing but clear away! Everything which even remotely smacked of mysticism and morality, of pietism and romanticism, or even of idealism, was suspected and sharply interdicted or bracketed with reservations which sounded actually prohibitive! What should really have been only a sad and friendly smile was a derisive laugh!

Did not the whole thing frequently seem more like the report of an enormous execution than the message of the Resurrection, which was its real aim?[42]

Where did we really go astray? . . . [There was a] deep-seated, essential infirmity in our thinking and speaking at that time. I believe it consisted in the fact that we were wrong exactly where we were right, that at first we did not know how to carry through with sufficient care and thoroughness the new knowledge of the *deity* of God which was so exciting both to us and to others.[43]

Who God is and what He is in His deity He proves and reveals not in a vacuum as a divine being-for-Himself, but precisely and authentically in the fact that He exists, speaks, and acts as the *partner* of man, though of course as the absolutely superior partner. He who does *that* is the living God. And the freedom in which He does *that* is His deity. It is the deity which as such also has the character of humanity. In this and only in this form was— and still is—our view of the deity of God to be set in opposition to that earlier theology. There must be positive acceptance and not unconsidered rejection of the elements of truth, which one cannot possibly deny to it even if one sees all its weaknesses. It is

[41] *Ibid.*, p. 41.
[42] *Ibid.*, p. 43.
[43] *Ibid.*, p. 44.

precisely God's *deity* which, rightly understood, includes his *humanity*.

How do we come to know that? What permits and requires this statement? It is a *Christological* statement, or rather one grounded in and to be unfolded from Christology. A second change of direction after that first one would have been superfluous had we from the beginning possessed the presence of mind to venture the whole inevitable counterthrow from the Christological perspective and thus from the superior and more exact standpoint of the central and entire witness of Holy Scripture. Certainly in *Jesus Christ*, as He is attested in Holy Scripture, we are not dealing with man in the abstract: not with the man who is able with his modicum of religion and religious morality to be sufficient unto himself without God and thus himself to be God. But neither are we dealing with *God* in the abstract: not with one who in His deity exists only separated from man, distant and strange and thus a nonhuman if not indeed an inhuman God.[44]

This critical scrutiny of his own thought, with which Barth has been concerned throughout his lifetime, brings him at the end of a half century of theological endeavor to an open and positive attitude that is both generous and comprehensive. If the divinity of God implies his humanity, nothing that is human can be irrelevant to God's witness. The faithful theologian discerns and accepts the whole created order as the work of a Creator who saw that it was "very good," and as the precious object of his love, for which he did not hesitate to sacrifice himself in Christ in order to restore it wholly to himself. When one smiles at the comparison of Barth's present affirmations with the vitriolic character of his early writings, he shakes his head and says in effect, "Please don't take for senility what is really the discovery and affirmation that the all-powerful love of God is the origin, *raison d'être* and ultimate goal of all things. Besides, could I really have come to where I am today if I had not begun as I did begin? *The Humanity of God* is not the negation but the fulfillment of the 'totally other' God of the first edition of *The Epistle to the Romans*."

[44] *Ibid.*, pp. 45–46.

MOZART

This "portrait" would be incomplete if we did not mention here, as an illustration of the above discussion, the place increasingly held by Mozart in Barth's life and thought. A well-known Mozart devotee, Barth begins each day by listening to one or two Mozart recordings, and he has written several articles on Mozart that have been well-received in musical circles. Thus when the two-hundredth anniversary of Mozart's birth was celebrated in May 1956, it was quite natural that the Basel committee organizing the commemorative ceremony should ask Barth to give the address. Between the second and third movements of the Serenade in C Minor for Wind Instruments (K. 388), Barth paid Mozart the highest tribute imaginable:

> Mozart's center is not like that of the great theologian Schleiermacher, identical with balance, neutralization and finally indifference. What happened in this center is rather a splendid annulment of balance, a *turn* in the strength of which the light rises and the shadow winks but does not disappear; happiness outdistances sorrow without extinguishing it and the "Yes" rings stronger than the still existing "No." Notice the *reversal* of the great dark and the little bright experiences in Mozart's life! "The rays of the sun *disperse* the night"—that's what you hear at the end of *The Magic Flute*. The play may or must still proceed or start from the very beginning. But it is a play which in some Height or Depth is winning or has already won. This directs and characterizes it. One will never perceive equilibrium, and for that reason uncertainty or doubt, in Mozart's music.[45]

His music mirrored real life in its two-sidedness, but in spite of that against the background of God's good creation and therefore, to be sure, always with a right turn, never with a left turn; this is

[45] Barth, "The Freedom of Mozart," in Walter Leibrecht, ed., *Religion and Culture: Essays in Honor of Paul Tillich*, Harper and Brothers, New York, 1959, pp. 76–77.

perhaps the meaning of his triumphant "charm." There is no shallowness, but no abyss either, in his music. He takes everything seriously. However, he never lets himself go nor does he allow himself to go beyond proper limits. He only says within limitations how everything is. Thus his music is beautiful, comforting, moving.[46]

In his "Letter of Thanks to Mozart," published by a Swiss journal, Barth had previously written:

If [one] really digests your musical dialectics he can be young and become old, he can work and relax, he can be gay and depressed; in short, he can live. You know now, far better than I, that much more is necessary for that purpose than the very best music. But there is much which helps men to this end (*ex post* and only incidentally!) and other music which cannot help toward it. Your music helps . . .

I have only a hazy feeling about the music played there where you now dwell. I once formulated my surmise about that as follows: whether the angels play only Bach in praising God I am not quite sure; I am sure, however, that *en famille* they play Mozart and that then also God the Lord is especially delighted to listen to them.[47]

THE "BIG BOOK"

We must not forget that during this whole troubled and involved period the various volumes of the *Church Dogmatics* were being published at an ever-increasing rate. The work expanded, widened in scope, occasionally slowed its pace and now and then got sluggish, much like a river making its way to the sea, but it displayed real maturity of thought, the highest sort of professional integrity, and was full of fresh insights. In 1945, with Volume III, Part I, Barth began his

[46] Barth, "Wolfgang Amadeus Mozart," in *op. cit.*, p. 68.
[47] Barth, "Letter of Thanks to Mozart," in *op. cit.*, pp. 63–64.

treatment of the doctrine of creation, which he radically reinterpreted; III/2 was published in 1948, III/3 in 1950, and III/4
in 1951. Then in 1953 IV/1 appeared, the crucial volume on
reconcilation, in which Christology is also discussed. IV/2 was
published in 1956, and IV/3 in 1959. Now well into his seventies, Barth briskly approaches the completion of IV/4 and occasionally smiles when explaining that he really doesn't need
to write Volume V (which will deal with eschatology or the
doctrine of the "last things"), since finally only the Lord himself, returning in glory, can write the final sentence, the real
conclusion, to all theological endeavor, which knows only
enough to outline and proclaim this point of convergence,
this omega of all human history.

PART THREE

A Critical Analysis of Barth's Principal Works

I. EXEGETICAL WORKS

Commentaries

We have already pointed out that Barth's full theological position is first expressed in the enormous commentary on *The Epistle to the Romans* (59). In it he made a balance sheet of all his theological knowledge; expressing himself in the language of his contemporaries, he found in this epistle (which had been so decisive for Luther) the arguments and emphases by which to demolish the theological positions of his own time, whether they were based on religious experience, religion, rationalism, piety or ethics. It was the strident clang of the bell announcing the death knell of all humanistic or sentimental theology. In it, because of Barth's extraordinary ability to translate Paul into a contemporary idiom, the reader hears the apostle speak like a twentieth-century man, not proclaiming slogans or principles or ideals for contemporary civilization or humanism—but the judgment of God. The gospel does not enthrone but rather condemns the efforts by which man endeavors to raise himself to God or merely to get higher than he was before. The apostle is a witness, not a genius, someone in whose radical defeat God's sole victory is manifested.

The second edition of *The Epistle to the Romans* was published in 1922. In the preface to this work, which was completely recast, Barth wrote:

> If I have a system, it is limited to a recognition of what Kierkegaard called the "infinite qualitative distinction" between time and eternity, and to my regarding this as possessing negative as well as positive significance: "God is in heaven, and thou art on earth."[1]

Commenting on this passage, Jean Bosc says:

> God, the God who speaks in the Bible, is the God who is on high in heaven, that is to say, far above the earth of men. The eye does not see him, the ear does not hear him, and knowledge of him does not increase in the heart of man. When man forgets that, when he believes somehow that he has God at his disposal, he moves into the world of "religion," that is to say into the world where man believes that he can place his hand upon God and touch him, while actually he is only replacing God with his own thoughts and desires and therefore with himself.[2]

Barth describes this kind of pretention in stinging terms:

> Woe be to us, if from the summits of religion there pours forth nothing but—religion! Religion casts us into the deepest of all prisons: it cannot liberate us. Flesh is flesh; and all that takes place within its sphere, every step we undertake towards God, is as such *weak*. Because of the qualitative distinction between God and man, the history of religion, Church History, is *weak*—utterly *weak*. Since religion is human, utterly human history, it is flesh, even though it be draped in the flowing garments of the "History of Salvation." *All flesh is grass* . . .[3]

[1] Barth, *The Epistle to the Romans*, preface to the second edition, Oxford University Press, New York, 1933, p. 10.
[2] Jean Bosc, *Karl Barth*, Editions Berger-Levrault, Paris, 1957, pp. 13–14.
[3] Barth, *op. cit.*, p. 276.

Bosc summarizes this emphasis in Barth as follows:

This sort of "religion" is the most radical form of sin, in spite of all its spirituality. Now the theology of the nineteenth century, in the midst of which Barth grew up, and which he studied, was guilty of this confusion between God and man. In that theology, the knowledge of God was too dependent on the experience of man; theology was too much identified with psychology; faith too identified with piety; man too much the subject of his relationship with God; and God too often made in the image of man.

The first task of theology, in the face of this, was therefore to emphasize and to respect the infinite distance between God and man. God is in heaven and man is on earth. God is the "Wholly Other," and man can be no more than the object of his concern. Only God can speak truly of God, and man can be the object of the divine grace only as a "void." "The importance of an apostle," Barth wrote, "is negative rather than positive. In him a void becomes visible." (Epistle to the Romans, p. 33)

As man, man is incapable of knowing God. The relationship of man with God can have only a single origin and a single direction. It comes vertically from above to below.[4]

Let us note finally that Barth has written a third and more easily available commentary on this Pauline epistle that has always been so influential in his thought. During the winter of 1940–41 he gave some extramural lectures at the University of Basel. The text of this concise commentary first appeared in mimeograph form, was then translated into several languages and finally appeared in English as *A Shorter Commentary on Romans.*[5]

Someone really ought to publish an edition of Barth's three commentaries on Romans, printed in parallel columns. In such a book the reader would be able to observe the development of Barth's thought, from the most abrupt phase of the "revelation" that had been given to him, up to the time when he wrote as simply as possible for the sake of readers with no

[4] Jean Bosc, *op. cit.*, p. 33.
[5] Published by John Knox Press, Richmond, Virginia, 1959.

theological training. Even more important, however, such a book would illustrate the way in which a theologian can listen to the criticisms of his opponents and appropriate them in his own thought. As we have already pointed out, the initial *Epistle to the Romans* was like a huge rock that Barth flung into the theological sea during the first quarter of the twentieth century. The second edition is completely different, for in it the reactions, criticisms and comments of his critics are acknowledged, and none of them are ignored or treated contemptuously. Even before he published the 1919 edition, Barth had entrusted the manuscript to Eduard Thurneysen, who read it pen in hand, writing comments in the margins, occasionally at great length. Barth, delighted by this, insisted that the publisher include Thurneysen's additions in the book itself, and slyly wrote in the preface, "In this way he has erected a hidden monument in my work." The 1922 edition benefited from the comments of the contemporary Protestant theological world and a number of Catholic theologians as well.

This is characteristic of Barth's theology. He is always in dialogue (and this is another example of his way of thinking dialectically[6]) with those who cross his path and take issue with him. Indeed, he takes those who disagree with him equally seriously, and the "pagans" have helped him more than once to understand the cosmic dimension and import of the gospel. If in 1919 the reader found himself confronted by a massive affirmation full of challenges and sheer confessionalism, by 1922 the surface of the work was broader and the voices heard within it were more diverse. The future riches of the *Church Dogmatics* can already be found in the second *Epistle to the Romans*. Barth teaches us, in a unique way, that a theologian cannot work by himself, and that he has no exclusive corner on the truth. Consequently, all work and research, if it is to be true to its subject matter, must be written

[6] See pp. 127–131 below, "A Note on Dialectical Method."

in a communal atmosphere and in an ecumenical spirit.[7] So Barth exemplifies a rather uncommon virtue: he knows how to hear and understand those who are furthest from him. His reply, no matter how unyielding and straightforward it may be, always begins with a genuine attempt to understand the point of view of the questioner, for dialogue always implies involvement with the one who, even in his opposition (and even in his mistakes), is always the mysterious messenger of Truth.

During 1940–41 the important thing in the midst of the Hitlerian torment was to nourish people, to give them some understanding of reasons for living that were more important than life itself. The third commentary on Romans, written at this time, is a substantial yet unpretentious piece of work, in which Barth achieves the almost impossible task of communicating the profound message of the apostolic letter, without distortion, in language that non-theologians can understand. Giving evidence of real teaching ability, he calls upon his readers to *read the text*; occasionally, as he explains various portions of the text, he seems to turn around and ask his hearer with a wink, "Isn't it really quite simple?"

The Resurrection of the Dead[8] is another comprehensive commentary. This is a study of 1 Corinthians 15, preceded by a long introduction on the epistle as a whole. This study is dependent on the work Barth did for *The Epistle to the Romans*, and in it the young teacher flexes his theological muscles on one of the most difficult and magnificent chapters in the whole New Testament.

A brief study on *The Nature of the Epistle of James* (106) appeared in 1927, in the Almanach des Chr. Kaiser-Verlags.

The Epistle to the Philippians,[9] originally published in 1927, is a balanced and gripping work that has since appeared in many editions and various translations, and has also

[7] See Barth's speech on "The Ecumenical Role of the Reformers" in a special issue of *Foi et Vie*, October 1948, devoted to the Amsterdam Conference.
[8] Published by Fleming H. Revell Company, New York, 1933.
[9] Published by John Knox Press, Richmond, Virginia, 1962.

been widely used in laymen's groups. Along with A _Shorter Commentary on Romans_, it is undoubtedly the most easily understood of Barth's exegetical works.

An Interpretation of Mark 13 (258), published in 1939 in the Swiss student journal _In Extremis_, is an extremely condensed commentary in which Barth, confronted by the impending outbreak of World War II, distinguished between things that are "the signs of the times" and things that are not, and made a rigorous distinction between eschatology and apocalypticism.

Christ and Adam[10] is a long study of the relationship between the first and second Adam as set forth in Romans 5. First published in 1952 in the journal _Theologische Studien_, it is much influenced by the sort of anthropological inquiry to which we have elsewhere called attention.

We must note further that the _Church Dogmatics_ is crammed with fine-print sections of exegesis and Biblical theology. This means that many who do not read every page of the _Dogmatics_ nevertheless refer to it frequently, either as a commentary or as a dictionary of Biblical theology. (The tables of contents, prepared under the supervision of Charlotte von Kirschbaum, are a great help in this connection.) A number of the volumes of the _Dogmatics_ are little more than huge commentaries accompanied by theological interpretation. III/1, for example, is an extended commentary on Genesis 1–2, while II/2 deals similarly with Romans 9–11.

Books of sermons

Barth has never forgotten that theology is at the service of the church as the dynamic, nourishment and corrective of its preaching, and he has continually made this clear by his own vigorous preaching. Even in his parish days at Safenwil he was publishing sermons (51, 53, 56). In 1918 he and Thurneysen

---

[10] Published by Harper and Brothers, New York, 1957, and Collier Books (paperback), New York, 1962.

together published a collection of sermons that reflects the intense theological investigation in which both men were then engaged, called *Seek God and You Shall Live* (58). In 1924 the two friends did the same thing again, publishing another volume, *Come, Holy Spirit*.[11] In 1935 they published their third joint volume, *God's Search for Man*,[12] containing sermons about maturity and inner peace, but even so related to the upheaval of the 1930s.

Later on, in 1949, a book was printed in Munich with the title *Fear Not!* (363). This volume includes sermons by Barth from 1934 in Bonn through 1948 in Debrecen, Hungary. In these sermons, notable both for their depth and integrity, a whole period in the life of the church is held up and illumined by the Word of God. There is no attempt at eloquence or sensationalism here; from the first page to the last, the Biblical text is expounded, and makes its impact by its sheer objective power and authority. Everything else is secondary.

It is worth noting that Barth, who no longer has a regular pulpit, frequently conducts worship at the main prison in Basel, preaching with touching simplicity to a large congregation about the gospel of freedom to the captives. He claims that in this situation he finds himself at ease, for the situation is completely unambiguous. Behind all the masks, man's true face is visible, each one as he actually is, a prisoner to whom the word of deliverance must be preached. To preach is to be the messenger charged with making this good news heard, to be the voice that conveys the liberating Word, the Word that only God himself can really declare, the Word that is none other than God himself become man in Jesus Christ. The personal ideas and idiosyncrasies of the preacher mean nothing at all in this situation. Unless God uses the preacher's words as a vehicle of his own Word, the sermon is meaningless and empty. Preaching is therefore the ever repeated expectation and risk that the miracle will occur by which God

[11] Published by Round Table Press, New York, 1933.
[12] Published by Round Table Press, New York, 1935.

will speak to men in our time, just as he has spoken to men in every time ever since the day when he called Abraham to set out for the promised land.

On Sunday morning when the bells ring to call the congregation and minister to church, there is in the air an *expectancy* that something great, crucial, and even momentous is to *happen*. How strong this expectancy is in the people who are interested, or even whether there are any people whatever who consciously cherish it, is not our question now. Expectancy is inherent in the whole situation.[13]

Speaking the word of God is the *promise* of Christian preaching. Promise is not fulfillment. Promise means that fulfillment is guaranteed us. Promise does not do away with the necessity of believing but establishes it. Promise is *man's* part, fulfillment is *God's*. We can only believe that what is God's is also man's. "We have this treasure in *earthen* vessels." No confusing of God's part with man's, of the treasure with the earthen vessel! No one indeed seems to confuse these two so easily as we theologians and careless philosophers, the very ones who ought to know better! But it is clear that even we can speak God's word if we can only believe. The word of God on the lips of a man is an impossibility; it does not happen; no one will ever accomplish it or see it accomplished. The event toward which the expectancy of heaven and of earth is directed is none the less *God's* act. Nothing else can satisfy the waiting people and nothing else can be the will of God than that he himself should be revealed in the event. But the Word of God is and will and must be and remain the word of *God*.[14]

Ought we, taking our stand against the world, against unchristian views of life, and against the unreligious masses, to have been flinging out accusations which we had not first applied in their full weight to our own selves—and applied so forcibly as to have squeezed out of us what breath we had for condemning others? Ought we to have been speaking of the sin *Eritis sicut Dei* [You shall be like God], without first having said each to himself: *Thou art the man, thou more than others?* And if we ought not, how

---

[13] Barth, "The Need of Christian Preaching," in *The Word of God and the Word of Man*, Harper and Brothers (Torchbooks), New York, 1957, p. 104.
[14] *Ibid.*, pp. 124–5.

can we but *be* under the judgement from which only the word of God can extricate and save us, as it can extricate and save *all* flesh? Our refusal to examine ourselves first can mean only that we are *not* satisfied with the promise, that we will *not* believe. How then can we hear and speak the word of God or our congregations learn to know and live it? How can anyone believe us? How can we preach the forgiveness of sins, the resurrection of the body, and the life everlasting—not merely in words but in reality?

We are *worthy* of being believed only as we are aware of our unworthiness. There is no such thing as *convincing* Christian utterance about God except as Christian preaching feels its *need*, takes up its *cross*, and asks the *question* which God demands in order to be able to answer it. From this need we may not hope to flee.[15]

Liberalism and pietism understood the sermon as the most personally individualistic act of Protestant worship. In Barth it receives a lofty objective reference, for Scripture and Scripture alone becomes its foundation, norm and content, the very framework within which it must be understood. When one returns to Barth's sermons with this in mind, he finds no attempt to be original, no desire to insinuate some new doctrine or point of view. Rather, what comes through to him is directness, precision and Biblical depth, based on the conviction that when the Biblical text is taken seriously the living voice of God can be heard within it today, and the only Word that is able to give men true freedom and true direction for their lives will sound forth.

From this follows a significant limitation: everything is disavowed that is not based on Scripture, and there is a constant return to Scripture as the only basis for true preaching, the only possible justification for the impossible task of preaching. It is particularly striking to notice that anxiety about the present state of affairs is *never* the point of departure for preaching, and yet how tumultuous have been the years in which Barth has preached! Preaching is never the speech of a Christian commentator on world affairs; the sole concern of

[15] *Ibid.*, pp. 128–129.

the preacher is for the Word of God, the Word that is eternal and therefore always contemporary. And when this is the case —but only when this is the case—it can happen that as a consequence the events of the day are occasionally clarified, put in proper context and taken to task, in the name of that Word and by its power. If the present situation, handled discreetly, intrudes into preaching, this is because that same Word leads it there and implies it. To do justice to this possibility, we must reclaim the word "prophetic." In the Old Testament, a prophet is a man who, if he does not predict the future, does proclaim the Word of God with utter concreteness for his own day and age, with all the implications that it can have for the society and politics of his time. There is no pietistic dualism here, as though the soul alone mattered; it is the *whole man* who is addressed, man with his concrete, material, historic and communal origins, man in his day-to-day existence. Similarly, the Word of God did not remain a theoretical idea; the Word was made flesh and became incarnate in Jesus Christ.

This, moreover, is why what is proclaimed is the "good news" of the deliverance, pardon and reconciliation that are freely given in Christ. It is not an abstract theory, not a speech about unreachable moral goals, full of reproach or accusation, but a message that gladdens, assists, strengthens and comforts. The gospel is never *against* men, it is always *for* men. This is why all true preaching is good to hear, helpful and full of light—like God's smile upon men, the Yes he addresses to the creatures whom he loves, the promise that one day the victory Christ won over death at Easter will be the only thing that counts, the eternal joy of all humanity finally delivered from sin and death.

We must repeat that it is not by chance that Barth prefers preaching to the inmates of the Basel prison. The most recent collection of his sermons, *Deliverance to the Captives*,[16] is moving testimony to this fact. Are we not all prisoners? Are

[16] Published by Harper and Brothers, New York, 1961.

we not all concerned with deliverance, whether we are inmates of prisons or so-called free men? All who recognize their solidarity with those in prison (both because Scripture so describes them in Hebrews 13:3 and because they know their own bondage from which only the grace of God can deliver them) will be particularly open to the message of these sermons. Since Jesus, in his sermon at Nazareth based on Isaiah 61, described himself as the "deliverer of the captives" (cf. Luke 4:16–22), a prison can certainly be the place of choice for witnessing and for meeting man in his true condition. It is clear that there also the gospel must be proclaimed in its full dimensions, as the message of the absolute grace of God who frees without conditions all men who are captives in their estrangement from him, and, having carried them over from death to life by the death and resurrection of his Son, calls them his friends and allows them to serve him. Neither rebuke nor condemnation nor dwelling upon the reasons for their sentence, but rather the good news of their unconditional deliverance—such is the message for which prisoners wait without knowing it, such is the only assurance that makes it possible for them to be free even in their prison cells and to remain free once their prison term has ended. Anyone who has preached the gospel to prisoners knows that this very unusual congregation forces him continually to return to the heart of the gospel—to the free love of God, to the forgiveness that makes all things new, to the Law of God, and to the description of the deliverance offered to all by the victory of grace. The real task of preaching, if it is trully based on the gospel, is nothing more and nothing less than proclaiming "deliverance to the captives."

Theology is important only as it restores the joyful note of genuine preaching to the church and the preacher. It is only by the content of the sermons it inspires that the real worth of a theology can be measured. It is by this basic test that Barth's work can and must be judged. Its most important result, which alone has real significance, is beyond any doubt the renewal of preaching that it has fostered throughout the world, from Germany to Japan, wherever dialectical theology has produced this new emphasis on the gospel that is Karl Barth's joy and love.

II. HISTORICAL WORKS

Barth has informed himself about the matters on which he speaks, and his critiques of the past and the present are not based on vague notions or expressed in flimsy generalities. It is with full knowledge of what is at stake that he takes his stand in the midst of the most diverse theological currents. Furthermore, the development of his own dogmatic position has always gone hand in hand with careful historical research. One of his first works, issued in Marburg in 1907, has the significant title *Modern Theology and the Task of the Kingdom of God* (7). In this essay Barth points out areas of agreement and divergence between the prewar theology and the new perspectives expressed particularly by the two Blumhardts.

In 1910 in Geneva Barth published a lively and relevant critique of the idealistic and pietistic theology and activity that at that time characterized *John R. Mott and the Student Christian Movement* (25).

The whole period of the writing and publishing of *The Epistle to the Romans* is marked by a continuing and fundamental encounter with the theological currents of the late nineteenth and early twentieth centuries. For example, in 1923 Barth published *Sixteen Answers to Professor Harnack* (77), and then several months later *An Answer to Professor Harnack's Open Letter* (80).

But there is space only to refer to such strictly historical works as the following: in 1920 *Ludwig Feuerbach*; in 1924 *Schleiermacher's "Celebration of Christmas"*; in 1925 *The Principles of Dogmatics according to Wilhelm Herrmann*; in 1926 *Schleiermacher*; in 1927 *The Word in Theology from*

Schleiermacher to Ritschl; in 1928 Roman Catholicism: a Question to the Protestant Church, the first of a series of studies on the Roman Catholic Church, which Barth knows thoroughly and with whose theologians he maintains an ongoing dialogue. All of these essays, along with several others, were published in Munich in 1928 as Theology and Church.[17] In 1931 came Anselm: Fides Quaerens Intellectum;[18] in 1933 Luther (168); in 1934 Schleiermacher (174); in 1936 The Church and the Oxford Group (205), a valuable critique, and Calvin (206); in 1939 David Friedrich Strauss (252); in 1947 the huge and exciting Protestant Thought: from Rousseau to Ritschl,[19] a full treatment of the various figures in Protestant theology since Schleiermacher, including a full treatment of their historical and cultural background and a notable introduction to the eighteenth century; Rudolf Bultmann: An Attempt to Understand Him[20] was published in 1952 at the height of the Bultmann controversy in Germany, and clearly states Barth's questions and reservations about Bultmann's thought.

In addition to these works, two other kinds of writing should be mentioned:

1. On the one hand, there are a considerable number of important historical sections in the Church Dogmatics. The indices of the various volumes give a helpful enumeration of the authors and works to which Barth has referred, indicating that he has never sought to theologize in a vacuum, but always in the contemporary situation and against the background of the history of theology and culture. To the degree that an actual question has already been asked and either well or badly answered, Barth puts it in historical perspective, thus treating it in its own context. The Church Dogmatics can rightly be appreciated as an extensive historical dictionary of

17 Published by S. C. M. Press, London, 1962.
18 Only recently published in English by John Knox Press, Richmond, Virginia, 1960.
19 Published by Harper and Brothers, New York, 1959.
20 In Hans Bartsch, ed., Kerygma and Myth, Volume II, S.P.C.K., London, 1962, pp. 83–132.

theology and culture, from their beginnings up to the present time.

2. On the other hand, there are various articles, lectures and memoranda which Barth has published, both on the struggle of the Evangelical Church under the Third Reich, and on the life of the churches under the communist regime since 1945, particularly in Hungary. Among these the following should be noted: *The Distress of the Evangelical Church* (142), *Protestantism at the Present Time* (152), *The Confessing Church in Nazi Germany* (198, and see also 200, 203, 211, 212, 213, 216, 218, 220, 221, 223–233), *The Christian Community in the Midst of Political Change: Documents of a Hungarian Journey*,[21] and *The Church and the Communist Regime in Hungary* (368).

There are thus two sides to Barth the historian: the scholar and the witness. But he is one or the other only as a Christian and a preacher. There can be no separation between these tasks, and the articulation of the historical and contemporary concerns of the church about its message has never been more obvious or connected than in Barth's case.

We must stress again that his historical method is above all characterized by a recognition of the strength of the position under examination; neither aloof objectivity nor censorious judgments, neither caricature nor unexamined presuppositions, are to be found in his writings. Barth the historian tries to be fair, to use the words of those whom he attacks so that they may speak for themselves, to point out the influences at work upon them and the subtleties and implications of their position, as well as the positive meaning and permanent worth of what they have affirmed. In his works of straight history he lets the reader draw his own conclusions; in the *Church Dogmatics* he becomes a penetrating and unprejudiced critic of the material under discussion. In the classroom Barth demonstrates the same kind of objectivity, the same respect for persons and ideas. Week after week, along with his students,

[21] In *Against the Stream*, S. C. M. Press, London, 1954, pp. 51–124.

he reads, and teaches them to read, the most diverse kinds of assignments, from Calvin to the Vatican Council, from Schleiermacher to Bultmann.[22]

The number, diversity and scope of these historical works (to which ought at least to be added unpublished works on Luther and Calvin) are sufficient to have justified the lifetime activity of a church historian. For Barth these are not merely preparatory or secondary works but also contributions to the ongoing ecumenical dialogue, apart from which he does not believe there can be true theology.

If from all these titles one had to choose two that were most characteristic of Barth's historical writing, these would surely have to be the study of Anselm, *Anselm: Fides Quaerens Intellectum*, the importance of which we have already noted, and *Protestant Thought: from Rousseau to Ritschl*. According to Henri Bouillard, S.J., a French specialist in Barth's theology, the book on Anselm occupies a place in Barth's thought similar to that occupied by the *Discourse on Method* in Descartes' writings.[23] Appearing several months before the publication of the prolegomena to the *Church Dogmatics*, I/1, this book marks the transition between the period of Barth's apprenticeship and his maturity, and one can understand Barth's affection for it, since it represents both a stage in his own development and a full introduction to his own distinctive theological position. The book deals with Anselm's proof of the existence of God, but before studying and commenting on the ontological argument Barth sits at Anselm's feet in order to learn from him what theology really is.

The knowledge, the *intellectus*, with which Anselm is concerned is the *intellectus fidei*. That means that it can consist only of positive meditation on the object of faith. It cannot establish this object of faith as such but rather has to understand it in its very incomprehensibility. Yet nevertheless, it has to progress at

[22] Translator's Note: It is worth noting in this connection that for two summers Barth has given a course at Basel on the theology of Paul Tillich.
[23] Translator's Note: Cf. Henri Bouillard, *Karl Barth, Genèse et Évolution de la théologie dialectique*, Aubier, Paris, 1957, p. 145.

the level of reflection, expressing in symbols what in itself cannot be expressed. It will therefore be able to claim only scientific certainty for its results and not the certainty of faith and it will therefore not deny the fundamental imperfection of these results. It will not on any account be able to set itself in explicit contradiction to the Bible, the textual basis of the revealed object of faith. And it would not be what it is or achieve what it does achieve if it were not the knowledge of faith-obedience. In the end, the fact that it reaches its goal is grace, both with regard to the perception of the goal and the human effort to reach it; and therefore in the last analysis it is a question of prayer and the answer to prayer.[24]

Having thus defined the nature of theology—and we cannot emphasize too much the relationship between prayer and the theological knowledge—Barth goes on to study the ontological argument, and, breaking with all the traditional philosophical interpretations, shows that it corresponds exactly to the procedure that Anselm had marked out, in the humble audacity of prayer.

Philosophers in many countries have given attention to this book, and it has given rise to some interesting discussions. In France, for example, the noted medieval scholar Étienne Gilson has commented on the clarifying nature of Barth's interpretation.

In Barth's second major historical work, the treatment of the nineteenth century called *Protestant Thought: from Rousseau to Ritschl,* he begins paradoxically by painting a brilliant picture of the *eighteenth* century, in what is without doubt the best single section of the book. Here again, before indulging in any critique he tries to do justice to what he is studying. The philosophy of the Enlightenment is presented to us in all its greatness, and within it we discover what eighteenth-century man was really like—so amazingly confident of his own powers, so certain of his mastery of the universe, so optimistic about his own future, that we can recognize him whether under the guise of a Rousseau, a Lessing, a Kant or a

24 Barth, *Anselm: Fides Quaerens Intellectum,* pp. 39–40.

Hegel. We are introduced to the nineteenth century through a series of portraits, the same ones that decorate the stairway of Barth's home, the great theologians from Schleiermacher to Ritschl, who appropriate the gains of the Enlightenment for Protestant theology. Here again each man is given his due: what else could he say, after all, except what he understood and believed? When Barth here and there makes a critical comment, it is only to ask in effect, "This is where we have come from; do we really want to go back? Shouldn't we be grateful that we can examine the work of the nineteenth century calmly, appropriating its gains and avoiding its errors?"

This is the path the church must walk. It need not ignore or despise its past, but can live in the present moment, giving thanks to the power of the living Lord who day by day, century by century, gives it whatever it needs so that it may be faithful to its calling. If we are occasionally inclined to criticize our fathers, let us try to do better than they did, and let us also realize that the day will come when our sons will judge us, just as we have judged our fathers. The important thing, therefore, is not to be satisfied that we are better than they, but to respond faithfully to whatever God has in store for us today.

III. DOGMATIC WORKS

In Barth, the exegete and the historian serve the needs of the dogmatician, but the dogmatician never assumes that on his own resources he can establish a true relationship between Scripture, church history and culture. Barth's concern with systematic theology is never speculative, but is always checked, dominated and surrounded by the presence of the Word of God and the living witness of the church.

The shorter works

Barth's first dogmatic work was undoubtedly *The Right-eousness of God* (52), written during World War I, in which, quite Lutheran at this point, he explained that to believe is "to decide in favor of the righteous God." This was followed by a great many systematic works, both large and small: *The Christian's Place in Society, Biblical Questions, Insights and Vistas, The Word of God and the Task of the Ministry*, all of which, along with several others, were collected and published in 1924 as *The Word of God and the Word of Man*.

In 1930, after many other essays, Barth published a work in collaboration with his brother Heinrich, a philosopher, *On the Doctrine of the Holy Spirit* (134). In 1935 came *Credo*,[25] an interpretation of the Apostles' Creed originally given as lectures to Dutch students, and *Gospel and Law*,[26] an important study of the relationship between grace and obedience, justification and sanctification. In 1936 appeared *The Election of God* (209), a small pamphlet taking strong issue with the traditional doctrine of predestination. In 1938 appeared *The Knowledge of God and the Service of God*,[27] an interpretation of the Scots Confession of 1560, given in Scotland as the Gifford Lectures. In 1943 appeared *The Faith of the Church*,[28] an interpretation of the Apostles' Creed according to Calvin's catechism, and *The Teaching of the Church Regarding Baptism*,[29] in which Barth radically challenges traditional doctrine and practice, and proposes that only those who are able to remember their baptism should be baptized. In 1947 appeared *Dogmatics in Outline*,[30] a course of lectures given to

[25] Published by Charles Scribner's Sons (The Scribner Library), New York, 1962.
[26] In *Community, State, and Church*, Doubleday and Company (Anchor Books), Garden City, New York, 1960, pp. 71–100.
[27] Published by Charles Scribner's Sons, New York, 1939.
[28] Published by Meridian Books, New York, 1958.
[29] Published by S. C. M. Press, London, 1948.
[30] Published by Harper and Brothers (Torchbooks), New York, 1959.

students at Bonn.[31] In 1948 appeared *Christian Doctrine According to the Heidelberg Catechism* (351), and in 1949 *Prayer*,[32] an interpretation of the Lord's Prayer according to the catechisms of the Reformation.

The above listing includes only a few titles from among the many dogmatic writings listed in the bibliography of Barth's works. And having made this choice, we realize how inadequate would be any similarly quick enumeration of works that deserve extended commentary. We must also emphasize that a number of these small works include brand new material and have far-reaching implications for the history of Christian theology. Their full impact has not yet been felt, and only later will it be possible to evaluate the impetus for reappraisal and new directions that one or another of these writings has furnished for evangelical theology.

It would be worth tracing the development of Barth's thought, in his understanding of the creeds of the church, through the successive interpretations he has given of them. From *Credo*, published at the beginning of the struggle of the Confessing Church in Germany, and dedicated to "all who stood, stand and will stand," to *Christian Doctrine According to the Heidelberg Catechism* (351), a journey of great spiritual depth can be discerned, characterized both by the constant desire to return to the heart of the church's gospel and by the wish to respond in clear-cut fashion to the great questions that are posed for the church by its confrontation with the world—heresy and paganism in all their civil, religious and aggressive manifestations.

We must notice also that throughout these writings we can distinguish *a role for the church*. For Barth the church is not first of all an institution established in the world with certain privileges that are acknowledged or challenged according to the circumstances of the moment. Rather, the church

[31] Translator's Note: Attention should be called here to an unfortunate and confusing misprint that is found in all English translations of this work. Lines 2–4 on page 27 should read: "Christian faith is not irrational, not antirational, not suprarational, but rational in the proper sense."
[32] Published by Westminster Press, Philadelphia, 1952.

is an *event*, an encounter, ever fresh and unexpected, in which God, making himself known to men, calls them together for praise, witness and service to their fellow men. That here and there the institution should be overthrown by events is to be expected, as the example of the German church and the churches in communist countries makes plain. Furthermore, for Barth the church is always first of all the community, the parish church, in which, in a given social and political situation, some men are conscious of the presence of the living Lord in their midst, and are concerned to be his representatives in their worship and even more in their daily life. It is Barth's experience and expectation that "the living community of the living Lord" continues to be made known in all the institutions—either through them or in spite of them. It is easy to see why this dynamic conception of the church (fully upheld by the affirmations of the gospel and the Reformers about the priesthood of all believers) has not gained many adherents either among the official representatives of the institutional church or in certain theological circles!

Among the various titles we have mentioned, special attention must be paid to three, in which Barth casts fresh light on the problems with which he is dealing:

1. In *Gospel and Law*, Barth reexamines both the Old Testament and St. Paul on the meaning of the Ten Commandments, showing that the latter were given to a free people to serve as a specific reminder to them of the nature of the freedom that was given them by God's miraculous intervention in their life and their deliverance from slavery in Egypt. Grace therefore precedes Law and shows that the Christian serves God because he is already saved, and not in order that he may be saved. This means a return to an ethic of gratitude, a characteristic of all Reformed theology since Luther's little book on *The Liberty of the Christian Man*.

2. In *The Election of God*, Barth breaks with the speculative doctrine of double predestination, which is found in its most unacceptable form in the final edition of Calvin's *In-*

stitutes. For Barth, on the contrary, election is the good news that we only know our condemnation in the cross of Christ, as a curse which we deserve but which by grace Christ bears on our behalf, just as in the glorification of Christ we receive the assurance that we are raised up from eternal death to attain the glorious liberty of the children of God. Predestination thus ceases to be the mystery of terror and resignation that has scandalized so many men, and becomes what it should never have ceased to be—a chapter of the *gospel*, the good news that in Christ God has fully provided for our destiny, revealing and communicating to us the assurance of a victory that rescues us from eternal damnation. It is worth recalling that Barth hesitated a long time over this and, contrary to his usual custom, reworked the whole chapter on election in the *Church Dogmatics* after he had finished it. It was Pierre Maury who indicated this new direction to Barth in a significant article on "Election and Faith," now available in *Foi et Vie*, 1956, No. 3, pp. 199–219.[33]

3. In *The Teaching of the Church Regarding Baptism*, Barth searches for a narrow path equally removed from the errors of the Baptists, for whom baptism must be the sign of individual conversion (man's decision being excessively emphasized to the detriment of the prevenience of sovereign grace), and the excesses of the believers in infant baptism (who hold that every child must be baptized, whatever the spiritual attitude of the environment in which he lives). With a daring that has not failed to stir up misunderstandings, Barth emphasizes the importance of the *psychological* development of the child. The latter must be able to understand what is being done to him—else why should baptism be administered to him, since he is not capable of taking in its meaning? But such considerations ought not to lead to a notion of "believer's baptism." The prevenience of grace must

[33] Translator's Note: This important article has apparently never been translated into English, but other writings of Maury on the subject are available in Pierre Maury, *Predestination, and Other Papers*, John Knox Press, Richmond, Virginia, 1960, with an appreciative foreword by Barth.

be maintained, and baptism must remain what it was in the early church, the sacrament of entrance into the faith.

This pamphlet, and the discussion which it precipitated, have contributed greatly to the reconsideration of the study of baptismal practice in various churches, particularly the Reformed Church of France, which, at the national Synod at Chambon-sur-Lignon in 1951, officially adopted a double baptismal practice.

The Church Dogmatics

All the above work, so widespread that we have barely touched the high spots, prepares for, centers upon and is fulfilled in the *Church Dogmatics*. This is a mammoth work, still unfinished, even though twelve volumes, totaling over six thousand pages, have actually been published.

When finished, the work will consist of five parts. At present (1962) it is in the last quarter of part four. The fifth and final part will deal with eschatology, under the heading of "the doctrine of redemption." Here is the general arrangement of the twelve volumes presently available:

I/1 and I/2 contain the *prolegomena* to the whole *Dogmatics*. They include an introduction to the work itself, and deal with the task, object, foundations, method and means of understanding theology in general and dogmatics in particular. Along with these are basic chapters on the doctrine of the Trinity (the objective starting point for all theology), Christology, the doctrine of the Holy Spirit and the doctrine of Scripture.

Volume II deals specifically with *the doctrine of God*:

II/1: The knowledge of God: the knowability of God and the limits of the knowledge of God; the reality of God and his perfections, such a love, freedom, omnipotence, wisdom, omnipresence, etc.

II/2: The doctrine of God's gracious election, and the command of God which forms the basis for Christian ethics.

Volume III deals with *the doctrine of creation:*

III/1: The basis of creation, the relationship between cove-nant and creation. (The whole volume, as we have already pointed out, is a detailed and lengthy exegesis of Genesis 1–2.)

III/2: The Christian doctrine of man, a theological anthro-pology.

III/3: The providence of God, the powers of Nothing-ness, and the angels.

III/4: Ethical problems growing out of man's status as a created being: the relationship with the created order, the re-lationship between man and woman, marriage, parents and children, near and distant neighbors, respect for life (i.e. sui-cide, sickness, capital punishment and war), work, vocation, dignity, honor, etc.

Volume IV deals with *the doctrine of reconciliation* of God and man in Jesus Christ:

IV/1: In Jesus Christ, the Son of God, who judges the liv-ing and the dead, humbles himself and identifies himself with man, who is condemned to judgment: the Lord becomes a servant (the *priestly* ministry of Christ). In the light of this fact sin is seen as essentially pride, and to this corresponds the judgment of God, which brings about the justification of the sinner. The latter is expressed, in human terms and by the action of the Holy Spirit, in the gathering of the Christian community and the birth of faith in every Christian.

IV/2: Jesus Christ is the exaltation of fallen man, who at-tains to life with God and for God: the servant becomes the Lord (the *kingly* work of Christ). In the light of this fact sin is seen as essentially sloth when confronted by the Word of God and his demands: the work of God continues in the sanctification of the justified sinner. The latter is expressed, in human terms and by the action of the Holy Spirit, in the upbuilding of the Christian community and the new life of the Christian in love.

IV/3 (1 and 2): In this volume (so long that it is divided into two parts) Barth completes his presentation in a way that makes its logical rigor and symmetrical architecture quite plain, by developing his thought along the lines set out at the beginning of IV/1: Jesus Christ is the guarantor and true witness of our reconciliation, the one in whom it is seen with full clarity (the *prophetic* work of Christ). In the light of this fact sin is seen as essentially falsehood, the denial of the truth, the rejection of the Word; the work of God in man, the victory of the Holy Spirit over man's sin of falsehood, is expressed in the sending forth of the Christian community and the life of the Christian in hope.

IV/4: This volume will deal with the ethics of reconciliation and will examine the doctrine of the sacraments in detail.

The *Church Dogmatics* is so large as to be almost grotesque. As we have already suggested, Barth in his later years resembles a stream whose rich delta stretches out to infinity. The reader is sometimes disconcerted and discouraged by the sheer weight of words and the difficulty of understanding the long German sentences. The translation of such a work is nearly impossible; one needs to learn German in order to appreciate all the nuances and penetrate to the innermost depths of this theological edifice. But it is well worth the effort! He who accepts the discipline of reading these nearly seven thousand pages finds an exciting world unfolding; amazed, fascinated and overwhelmed, he simply cannot tear himself away from these huge volumes with their disciplined structure, their details and their long sections in fine print. The reader enters into this thought world and it enters into him, calling forth from him not slavish imitation but an echo full of new sounds and unexpected overtones.

We have here, in other words, a theological achievement of the first order, a summation of contemporary evangelical thought. Historical parallels are always dangerous and are likely to boomerang, but for those who come to terms with the *Dogmatics*, Barth takes his place in the succession of the great teachers of the church, such as Augustine, Aquinas, Luther and Calvin.

We have already commented on the paradoxical fact that (at least at the present time) the non-Protestants are the ones most aware of Barth's importance, and those who take most seriously what he has done. If historical parallels are dangerous, historical predictions are even more so; nevertheless we are certain that the future will recognize Barth's importance even more than the present does. This has always been the case with theologians who return to the sources and rediscover the authentic Biblical message: their detractors have never caught up with them, and their work has remained significant. If Otto Dibelius is right in his assertion that the twentieth century will have been for Protestantism "the century of the church," in the theological realm this will have been underscored decisively by the work of Karl Barth and his *Dogmatics* in particular.

Of all the sciences, theology is the most beautiful, the one that touches the mind and heart most profoundly, the one that approaches human reality most closely and offers the clearest vision of the truth all science is seeking, the one that comes closest to what is really meant in university life by the honored and profound word *Fakultät*, a landscape with a far-distant perspective that is nevertheless bright, like those of Umbria or Tuscany, or a work of art as wonderful and yet as strange as the cathedrals at Cologne or Milan. Poor theologians and poor theological eras which, strangely enough, have not taken account of all that beauty!

But among all the sciences, theology is also the most complicated and the most dangerous. It is the one that, when one is involved in it, can lead very quickly to despair or, what is almost even worse, to pride. It is the one that, losing itself in flights of fancy or becoming petrified, can, worst of all, become its own caricature. Is there any science that can become as monstrous and as boring as theology? That man is no theologian who has never shuddered in fear before its abysses or has ceased to be terrified by it.

Both of these things are true and each has its cause in the fact that theology does not need, cannot and is not allowed to justify its existence, its necessity, its work and its results. It is the most free and also the most bound of all the sciences. All the questions that are asked about its right to exist it can quite simply refer to the church and to the divine revelation on which the church is based—that is to say the life of the Christian which moves from baptism to the Lord's Supper, from the claim "Jesus Christ has come" to the claim "Jesus Christ will come again."[34]

"Jesus Christ has come, Jesus Christ will come again"— these are the two limits of the parenthesis within which dogmatics is born and lives, a basic function of the church that must always reflect upon its message and state it as clearly as possible.

[The Church] is the place, the community, charged with the object and the activity with which dogmatics is concerned, namely the proclamation of the Gospel. By calling the Church the subject of dogmatics we mean that where dogmatics is pursued, whether by pupil or by teacher, we find ourselves in the sphere of the Church. The man who seeks to occupy himself with dogmatics and deliberately puts himself outside the Church would have to reckon with the fact that for him the object of dogmatics would be alien, and should not be surprised if after the first steps he could not find his bearings, or even did damage.[35]

Dogmatics will always be able to fulfill its task only in accordance with the state of the Church at different times. It is because the Church is conscious of its limitations that it owes a reckoning and a responsibility to the good it has to administer and to cherish, and to the good One who has entrusted this good to it. It will never be able to do this perfectly; Christian dogmatics will always be a thinking, an investigation and an exposition which are relative and liable to error. Even dogmatics with the best knowledge and conscience can do no more than question

[34] Translator's Note: In Barth, "Offenbarung, Kirche, Theologie," in *Theologische Fragen und Antworten*, Evangelischer Verlag AG, Zollikon-Zürich, 1957, p. 175. The last three lines of the above translation are not included in the German text, but are part of the French translation which M. Casalis was following.
[35] *Dogmatics in Outline*, pp. 9–10.

after the better, and never forget that we are succeeded by other, later men; and he who is faithful in this task will hope that those other, later men may think and say better and more profoundly what we were endeavouring to think and to say. With quiet sobriety and sober quietness, we shall do our work in this way. We must use our knowledge as it has been given to us to-day. No more can be required of us than is given to us. And like a servant who is faithful in little, we must not be sorrowful about such little. More than this faithfulness is not required of us.

As a science dogmatics takes account of the content of proclamation in the Christian Church. There would be no dogmatics and there would perhaps be no theology at all, unless the Church's task consisted centrally in the proclamation of the Gospel in witness to the Word spoken by God. This task, which rises up again and again, this problem put to the Church from the beginning, the problem of instruction, doctrine, witness, proclamation, really stands as the question, not just for parsons and theologians, but again and again before the Church as a whole: What as Christians do we really have to say? For undoubtedly the Church should be the place where a word reverberates right into the world. Since the Church's task is to proclaim the Word spoken by God, which is still at the same time a human work, theology and what we today—practically since the seventeenth century—term dogmatics have been necessary from the beginning.[36]

Thus it is clear that dogmatics is the work of the whole church, the community of believers, not simply of the clergy or the institution but the work of all believers in Christ, who know that they are responsible together for Christian witness, or more precisely, for preaching the Word of God. For Barth every Christian is an influential theologian, called to take part in the ministry of the church in the world. Barth's *Dogmatics*, however technical and specialized it may be, is not a theology for clerics, but material intended for the inner life of all the people of God, with which all the laity[37] are called upon to associate themselves.

[36] *Ibid.*, pp. 11–12.
[37] It should be remembered that "laity" comes from the Greek *laos*, meaning "people."

Furthermore, we must repeat that the *Dogmatics* is fully open to the world; not only is the voice and work of professional theologians to be found within it, but the preoccupations and concerns of laymen and nonbelievers are also considered. In a well-known section of the *Dogmatics* Barth emphasizes that the church's preaching of the Word of God necessitates an authentic dialogue with non-Christians, for he believes that the history of the people of God is a kind of parenthesis in the overall history of mankind, so that each is involved in the other and neither can be understood apart from the other. This means that Christians may not evangelize or teach the "others" from the height of their superiority; their witness presupposes a true encounter, a dialogue in which each approaches the other on the basis of full equality, listens to what the other has to say and learns something from the encounter. The Church that believes in the Lordship of Jesus Christ over the whole world ought to be able to listen to what the Lord says to it through the voices of the pagans whom he rules:

If we know the incarnation of the eternal Word and the glorification of humanity in Him, we cannot pass by any other man, without asking whether in his humanity he does not have this mission to us, he does not become to us this compassionate neighbor.[38]

But the thing that makes Barth's theology most distinctive and revolutionary is the centrality given to *the doctrine of Christ*, not only in Volume IV, but in all the preceding volumes.

It is believed that the original Christian Confession consisted of the three words, "Jesus Christ [is] Lord," to which were only later added the first and third articles. This historical event was not arbitrary. It is also materially significant to know that historically the second article is the source of the whole. A Chris-

[38] *Church Dogmatics*, I/2, p. 426.

tian is one who makes confession of Christ. And Christian confession is confession of Jesus Christ the Lord.

Starting with this heart of the Christian Confession, all that it expresses of God the Father and God the Holy Spirit is to be regarded as an expanding statement. When Christian theologians wished to sketch a theology of God the Creator abstractly and directly, they have always gone astray, even when in tremendous reverence they tried to think and speak of this high God. And the same thing took place when the theologians tried to push through a theology of the third article, to a theology of the Spirit, to a theology of experience as opposed to the theology of the high God in the first article . . .

Starting with Jesus Christ and with Him alone, we must see and understand what in the Christian sense is involved by the mighty relationship, to which we can only point again and again in sheer amazement, about which we cannot help being in danger of great error, when we say, *God and man.* What we mean by that can only be declared adequately, by our confession that "Jesus is Christ." And as for what is involved in the relationship between creation and the reality of existence on the one hand, and on the other hand the Church, redemption, God—that can never be understood from any general truth about our existence, nor from the reality of history of religion; this we can only learn from the relation between Jesus and Christ. Here we see clearly what is meant by "God *above* man" (Article I) and "God *with* man" (Article III). That is why Article II, why Christology, is the touchstone of all knowledge of God in the Christian sense, the touchstone of all theology. "Tell me how it stands with your Christology and I shall tell you who you are." This is the point at which ways diverge, and the point at which is fixed the relation between theology and philosophy, and the relation between knowledge of God and knowledge of men, the relation between revelation and reason, the relation between Gospel and Law, the relation between God's truth and man's truth, the relation between outer and inner, the relation between theology and politics. At this point everything becomes clear or unclear, bright or dark. For here we are standing at the centre. And however high and mysterious and difficult everything we want to know might seem to us, yet we may also say that this is just where everything becomes quite simple, quite straightforward, quite childlike. Right here in this centre, in which as a Professor of Systematic Theology I must call to you, "Look! This is the point now! Either knowledge, or the greatest folly!"—here I am in front of you, like a teacher in Sunday school facing his kiddies, who has something to say which a mere four-year-old can really understand. "The world was lost, but Christ was born, rejoice, O Christendom!"[39]

Since dogmatics is the indispensable work of the *Christ*ian church, exploring and formulating the *Christ*ian faith in systematic and critical fashion, with a view to *Christ*ian witness in the world, this implies that dogmatics must be, first, last and always, *Christology* and only Christology, that it must be constantly and invariably Christological. This follows the moment one takes the adjective "*Christ*ian" seriously, not as a mere label, but as a way of describing the objective reality from which the Church's faith and witness are nurtured. And this is precisely what Barth affirms:

A church dogmatics must, of course, be Christologically determined as a whole and in all its parts, as surely as the revealed Word of God, attested by Holy Scripture and proclaimed by the Church, is its one and only criterion, and as surely as this revealed Word is identical with Jesus Christ. . . . As a whole, i.e. in the basic statements of a church dogmatics, Christology must either be dominant and perceptible, or else it is not Christology.[40]

In 1933 Barth decided not to continue the course he started in the prolegomena to the 1927 *Christian Dogmatics*, and replaced this with the first "part-volume" of his *Church Dogmatics*. He had to do this in order to stress, as he put it, an unavoidable *Christological concentration*. For, as he discovered, "One cannot subsequently speak Christologically, if Christology has not already been presupposed at the outset."[41] Nothing in theology can be systematized or considered simply on its own; theology is only possible "if one has the person of Jesus Christ constantly before him."

[39] *Dogmatics in Outline*, pp. 65–67.
[40] *Church Dogmatics*, I/2, p. 123.
[41] *Ibid.*, I/2, p. 114.

This implies a lasting break with Catholicism and neo-Protestantism,[42] for each in its own way is guilty of having introduced or tolerated something exterior that upsets and destroys its theology. Wherever a second source of Christian knowledge has stood alongside Christ (whether it be reason, ethics, religious experience, history or science), theology has been turned aside from its main concern, which is the message of the apostles and prophets found within the Bible. For Scripture is the collection of testimonies made to Christ by the only authorized witnesses, the book whose authority is imposed on the church, and consequently on dogmatics, as the only valid and incontestable point of reference. Barth never forgets the example of the "German Christians," whose heresy consisted precisely in the fact that they acknowledged, in German history and in the "providential man" Adolf Hitler, a witness to revelation alongside Holy Scripture.

The "Christological concentration," therefore, is not a postulate formulated in arbitrary fashion by a rather original theologian. It is simply an inevitable way of expressing *obedience* and *gratitude*, of recognizing that Scripture leads us constantly to Christ and that Christ returns us constantly to Scripture. The *Dogmatics* thus conforms to the reality of revelation. Consequently, everything is rigorously Christological from beginning to end.

As far as the starting point of the *Dogmatics* is concerned, neither human values nor general epistemological considerations form the introduction to Barth's theology; he does not lay down a wide base from which to mount, step by step, to the God of Jesus Christ. On the contrary, following Anselm, with whom he basically agrees, Barth asserts that it is from believing, and from believing alone, that understanding proceeds; dogmatics is the work, consequence and obedience of faith, of faith alone. This is why, once the definitions have been established, it is "the doctrine of the Word of God" (I/1) that is expounded—the "Written Word" in the Bible, which sends us back to the "Word of God as preached" by

---

[42] Translator's Note: The latter is the term Barth uses throughout the *Dogmatics* to describe what we would call "Protestant liberalism."

the authentic witnesses, which has no other content and reference than the "Revealed Word," the event of revelation itself, which is the birth, life, death and glorification of Jesus Christ, the Son of God become man, the Word made flesh. He is the center of everything, the constitutive event of faith, Scripture and church. How could this event fail to be the pole around which all dogmatic thought revolves?

Because it deals primarily with this event of the revelation in Christ, the *Dogmatics* necessarily contains a long exposition of *the doctrine of the Trinity* (I/1), the keystone of any theology of revelation, since the God who gives himself to us in his revelation is himself love, from all eternity encounter and fellowship. His creating, reconciling and redeeming work reflects the threefold decision of his own inmost being, in the diversity of Father, Son and Holy Spirit. His revelation can only be a revelation of his unfathomable being, the manifestation of his grace, the expression of his mercy, the source of all reconciliation and of all true fellowship. This is why the gospel is *good* news, why theology is the investigation and expression of the greatest joy that man is capable of receiving. In order to see concretely how this fundamental point of view is expressed, one must turn to the *Dogmatics* itself and follow it through its long, and occasionally too long, outworking.

Within its carefully ordered structure, the *Dogmatics* presents a lasting and sometimes surprising interpretation of Christ and his work. Particularly impressive in the *humility* to which it witnesses—to the degree that it is inspired solely by the obedience of faith—it also exhibits a constant attitude of *adoration* which the reader cannot fail to perceive. The reader finds himself not only captivated by the sheer content of the pages but also deeply moved by their constant preaching, which is always centered on the good news of the reconciliation achieved by God in Christ.

Among the many surprising sections that radically challenge traditional theological positions, particular attention should be directed to those dealing with *election* (II/2). In contrast to the usual speculation about predestination, Barth focuses the whole Biblical witness in two finely etched theses: "Jesus Christ is the electing God," and "Jesus Christ is the elected man." In him we perceive both God's sovereign choice in uniting himself to humanity and the radical deliverance that proceeds from it for the sinful man who is mortally condemned. In this we recognize the *election of God*. Similarly, *ethics* is expressed in man's life as "the glorious liberty of the children of God," which has been restored to us by the reconciling work of Christ. Far from being a form of casuistry or a mechanical application of fixed principles, ethics is a continuous and free discovery, expressing the Christian life, which is the action of the living Christ in man, in each new situation. Here *gospel and law* can be seen clearly for what they truly are.

In Barth's treatment of *anthropology* the understanding of man and the discovery of his true meaning come only through faith in Christ, the new Adam (III/1).

Paradoxically, it is in *Christology* itself that the "Christological concentration" is most completely rethought. Whereas the order of systematic theology traditionally followed that of the "history of salvation" (e.g., creation, sin and reconciliation), in Barth's Christology reconciliation in each of its phases *precedes* the discussion of the corresponding phase of the doctrine of sin.[43]

We thus arrive at a carefully worked out correlation between the person of Christ (successively presented as he who humbles himself, he who is exalted and he who witnesses to our reconciliation) and his work (presented as deliverance from sin, which manifests itself as pride, sloth and falsehood). But above all, due to the fact that we discover the nature of sin only afterward, as the shadow cast by the light of Christ, the *Dogmatics* rightly expresses the content of the gospel: in reality we understand our sin only as those who are already pardoned, and our damnation only as the abyss from which the Savior Christ has already removed us. This

[43] See the discussion above on p. 105.

means that there can be no knowledge preliminary to, or separate from, Christ. We truly understand the world, history and mankind only as they are illumined by the divine person and work, which in Jesus Christ is revealed to us as the heart of the good news.

The implications of this methodological revolution are far-reaching. As Jacques de Senarclens has rightly emphasized, those whom Barth has guided back onto the path of a properly oriented dogmatics are not merely to repeat the lessons they have learned.[44] Barth's own work carries within it an invitation to surpass it. It achieves its end only when theologians, conscious of the demands that this "Christological concentration" implies for their own work, subject themselves to the same discipline—identical, incidentally, with the *sola Scriptura* of the Reformation—and apply it with humility and respect to every area of the thought, teaching, preaching and life of the church.[45]

[44] "La Concentration Christologique," *Antwort*, Evangelischer Verlag AG, Zollikon-Zürich, 1956, pp. 190–207.

[45] For those who have not read the *Dogmatics*, attention may be called here to the significant work by Otto Weber, *Karl Barth's Church Dogmatics*, Westminster Press, Philadelphia, 1954. The book digests the seven thousand pages of the *Dogmatics* down to about two hundred and forty pages, and is thus a reduction to about a thirtieth of the whole. It must be pointed out that the reader will find here only an analysis and a skeleton helping him to understand the structure and main outlines of Barth's mammoth work; it does not make unnecessary the reading of the original text, if one is to discover the facets, understand the nuances, and get into the main stream that runs from one end to the other. Here is Barth's comment on Weber's book:

"I look upon his work as an outline map of an area of the *Church Dogmatics* which has already grown so large. It could also be fittingly compared to the service of one of those well-made, valiant little tugs which may be seen in the great harbors of the world towing the somewhat out of proportion and cumbersome transatlantic steamers out into the open sea or into a safe port. For a long time I have realized that my understanding needs such a service. Certainly I myself would no longer have come to write a "Compendium" along with the "*Summa*," a "Medulla medullae" beside the "*Medulla*." Otto Weber, pursuing his own methods and of his own accord, has now ingeniously achieved something like this. I am obliged to him for doing it, and readers will also be. The possibility of the misuse of such a book is obvious. I think of lazy people who are always in a hurry to get things done, the glib talkers and superficial writers on this and the yon sides of the Atlantic, who, if possible will merely scan through even this compendium." (Barth, in the "Foreword to German Edition" of Weber, *op. cit.*, p. 10.)

IV. POLITICAL AND LITERARY WORKS

Political works

As we have already emphasized on more than one occasion, Barth is a theologian who is "involved." He takes the world and its daily life, even outside the confines of the church, with utmost seriousness. Is it not the place where Christ reigns invisibly and makes himself known? Is it not the place where the Word of God makes its impact, wherever the church understands that it does not exist for itself but for the world in which it is placed? We therefore find in Barth's work certain writings that are distinctively political, if this word is understood in its etymological and highest sense as concern for what happens in the city of man.[46]

As early as 1911 Barth was writing in this vein: *For the Dignity of Geneva!* (28) appeared in that year. In the same year, on a much more serious theme, he wrote *Jesus Christ and the Social Movement* (30), and *A Reply Concerning Military Airplanes* (35). In 1914 he wrote some articles on gambling and roulette (44, 45, 54), and in 1919 issued a solemn *Warning to the Citizens of Aargau* (60). Other writings of Barth, mentioned previously, were written after World War I. In these he writes from the standpoint of a theology

Thus, it is to the text itself that one must go to find out what it contains.

Translator's Note: The entire twelve volumes thus far published are now available in English, under the imprint of T. & T. Clark, Edinburgh, thanks to the diligent efforts of a group of Scottish translators headed by Professors G. W. Bromiley and T. F. Torrance. Another handbook similar to Weber's has recently appeared in English, *Karl Barth: Church Dogmatics, A Selection* with Introduction by Helmut Gollwitzer, translated and edited by G. W. Bromiley (Harper and Brothers [Torchbooks], New York, 1962). This contains longer passages from the original, arranged topically, whereas Weber's book is a kind of running paraphrase.

[46] Translator's Note: This is apparently a reference to the fact that the French *politique* can be traced back to the Greek *politēs*, meaning "citizen."

specifically involved in the events of the day, and combines his dogmatic rigor with a precise understanding of the world and with points of view as justified as they are explicit. In 1920 he wrote *The Christian in Society* (64); in 1922 *Basic Questions Concerning Social Ethics* (72); in 1923 *The Ethical Problem in the Present Day* (79). Then, after a plunge into pure theology, he wrote *Work as a Problem in Theological Ethics* (140) in 1931.

Following this come all the articles related to the German church struggle, articles that were certainly spiritual and yet eminently political at the same time, and gave ample reason for Barth and his friend Niemöller to be described as the two most dangerous enemies of the Third Reich. In 1938 came the important pamphlet *Church and State*,[47] in which Barth breaks once and for all with the political dualism of the Lutherans. He points out that God's work, conceived as a work of justice (in which the love of the just God vindicates the life of the sinner), implies that totalitarianism cannot govern the relationships between men, but must always be bound, corrected and restrained by law and justice. This pamphlet exhibits a fresh and important evangelical reflection on the relationship of church and state, the nature of the state, the significance of the state for the church, and the service the church should render to the state.

Another title from about the same time clearly shows Barth's attitude during these decisive moments in European history: *Once More We Ask—Peace or Justice?* (241). This article appeared in the *Kirchenblatt für die reformierte Schweiz* in 1938, and reminded Christendom in the Munich era that reasons for living could be much more important than life itself—a conviction little shared at the time. At the time of the Czech crisis, and then after the war began, various articles appeared, which in their published form furnish one of the best handbooks available on practical political ethics.[48]

[47] In *Community, State, and Church*, pp. 101–148.
[48] These wartime "letters" to Hromadka and others are preserved, along with other articles, in *Eine Schweizer Stimme*, 1938–1945, Evangelischer Verlag AG, Zollikon-Zürich, 1945.

The Christian Community and the Civil Community,[49] to which we have given considerable attention, dates from 1946 and represents such a balanced synthesis and fully worked out position that it is a helpful summary of political theology.

Next come the various articles about the churches on the other side of the Iron Curtain, to which we have also made many references. But we must note the article in 1950 on *The Church as a Factor in Political Education* (375) and the important issue of *Theologische Existenz heute* in 1952, which raised a basic question about *Political Decision in the Unity of the Faith*.[50] What does membership in a spiritual community imply for the civic and political activity of Christians when the existence of that community can be jeopardized, and its unity threatened, by the divergent decisions of its members?

But what sort of a Christian fellowship would it be where such things were not feasible and bearable? Indeed, how could it be a Christian fellowship living in expectation of its Lord, journeying on its way towards Him, if such things did not in fact take place —hard as they may be for all concerned? It is through such happenings that the Christian fellowship grows. . . . The decision of individual Christians—including the political decisions under discussion today—can and must take place, with all their consequences, within the unity of the faith, which can only be the unity of the Christian and the Evangelical faith if it has a dynamic character.[51]

The unity of the faith can maintain its spiritual truth and reality only by constant renewal. It can and will be renewed only if Christians do not try to avoid crises in their fellowship with one another, but are determined, whatever the outcome, to see them through. And let us not forget our point of departure: in practice the Church can choose only between using its political responsibility and thereby exposing itself to the risk of crises, and sparing itself the crises and thus failing to do justice to its political mission.[52]

49 In *Community, State, and Church*, pp. 149–189.
50 In *Against the Stream*, pp. 147–164.
51 "Political Decision in the Unity of the Faith," in *op. cit.*, p. 157.
52 *Ibid.*, p. 159.

It is clear that in most of the articles of this period the *Jewish question* is cited as the test case of Christian faithfulness: how could the people of God possibly disengage themselves from Israel?

We have already emphasized the historical importance of Barth's political writings, but their true significance is theological. It is evident from the above that Barth approaches all problems, the most unforeseen and the most pressing, from a clear theological perspective, and that nothing is more basic than this Barthian search for a Christian point of view in the present time. It is clear that in these writings Barth explicitly parts company with pietism, and also rejects the more or less romantic humanism of the social gospel. The political judgments a Christian makes are no more autonomous than those he makes elsewhere, for all that the Christian is, does and plans must be subordinated to the sovereign criterion of the Word of God.

If, therefore, Barth's political judgments and attitudes sometimes seem debatable to us, if here as elsewhere he encourages us, with humor and humility, to go further and to do better than he has done, his basic approach to these matters remains helpful to those who, today and tomorrow, are concerned with making the gospel relevant to the problems of the modern world. The basic theology of the incarnation, which Barth develops and expounds, is incomplete apart from its expression in the world of men.

Literary works

In the title of this section reference is made to literary works, most of which have already been mentioned in the preceding pages. *Protestant Thought: from Rousseau to Ritschl*, with its masterful estimates of the eighteenth and nineteenth centuries, the brief essays on Mozart and the voluminous fine-print sections of the *Dogmatics*, represent a scope of literary production that would make most critics green with envy. We must say once more that Barth's training and intelligence defy description. One can hardly ever call attention (as, for example, in his critique of Sartre) to a point of view too cursory or too negative; such writings are independent of Barth's theological work, complete in themselves, and yet they are at the service of the whole.

Any "portrait" of Barth ought to include some anecdote that would show how important humor and laughter are in his life. Let us recall that Barth has a sure poetic instinct and that, though he has never published a collection of poems, he intersperses little bits of verse in his correspondence and in the notes he takes during the boring meetings he must often attend. In *Antwort*, the volume of tributes published for Barth's seventieth birthday, Eduard Thurneysen quotes two of Barth's poems, the spirit and style of which can only imperfectly be captured in translation:

Barth wrote as follows in 1916:

As pilgrims among others we do intend
To be persistent in our own way.
Then, as we go, most likely we shall prove
The advantage of long-windedness.

But in 1926 he corrected the poem in the following way:

As pilgrims among others we intended
To be persistent in our own way.
But as we went, we too found ourselves
Beset by shortness of breath.

We wander now in mid-day heat.
No longer is there so much laughter.
And many a weapon that once we used
Is now as blunt as blunt can be.

There are times when the dear God lets us
"Be persistent in our own way."
But then the shadowed side appears,
Then comes the needful moderation.

But this moderation should not lessen
Our better confidence in wandering:
The old light shines steadily anew,
It shines for sinners, it shines for children.[53]

V. THE ECHO

Throughout this study we have emphasized the universal importance of Barth's work. On the occasion of his seventieth birthday this fact was attested to by testimonials coming from all over the world, as well as by the appearance of the *Festschrift* from which the above poem is taken. The table of contents in *Antwort* lists seventy-eight authors from twelve different countries, and the bibliography cites twenty-four translations into English (including the *Dogmatics*), twenty into French (including the *Dogmatics*), eighteen into Japanese (including a part of the *Dogmatics*), nine into Hungarian, seven into Czechoslovakian, ten into Danish, three into Swedish, three into Korean, two into Italian, one into Norwegian and one into Spanish.[54]

Apart from the translations, it is the theological journals in the various countries that are most under the influence of Barthian theology. As we have already emphasized, Roman Catholic circles have discovered Barth, and by means of critical articles and appraisals accord him a hearing that no other Protestant theologian of the past or present has ever known. The works of the French Jesuit Henri Bouillard[55] and of the Swiss-German priests Hans Urs von Balthasar[56] and Hans

[53] Translator's Note: This translation was prepared by James D. Smart for inclusion in a collection of letters exchanged by Barth and Thurneysen, which he is translating and editing for publication by John Knox Press. The original is in *Antwort*, p. 838.

[54] Translator's Note: The bibliography in *Antwort* includes no works published later than 1955. Since that time further works by Barth, and translations of his work, have continued to appear at an astonishing rate.

[55] *Karl Barth*, I: *Genèse et Évolution de la Théologie dialectique*; II and III: *Parole de Dieu et existence humaine*, Aubier, Paris, 1957.

[56] *Karl Barth: Darstellung und Deutung seiner Theologie*, Verlag J. Hegner, Köln, 1951. This work, long out of print, was reissued in 1962.

Küng[57] are, along with the work of the Dutch Reformed theologian G. C. Berkouwer,[58] the best treatments of Barth.

As can be seen from the publication dates of these latter works, the echo, far from getting feebler, continues to get louder, and is beginning to have a truly ecumenical resonance. Actually, the task of understanding, assimilating and utilizing the riches in Barth's work has scarcely begun, for the present generation consists of pupils who are often too fawning, and of critics who are often too jealous or superficial. Only the future can fully reveal the importance of Barth's contribution, although it can already be said that it has left its mark on the twentieth century.

Time will do its work, lessening the impact and present interest of the whole, while putting the different parts of Barth's work in perspective and assigning them their proper place in history. But one thing is clear. Barth is and will remain the theologian who rediscovered the message of the sovereign grace of God in Jesus Christ and forced the church to hear that message at a crucial moment in its life. He stressed the inevitable implications that flow from that message for the life of the Christian who is called by his Lord to be a true man, fully involved in the world and acutely conscious of all the problems that are posed for men by the troublesome questions of their earthly destiny.

[57] *Rechtfertigung*, Johannes Verlag, Einsiedeln, 1957.
[58] *The Triumph of Grace in the Theology of Karl Barth*, William B. Eerdmans Publishing Company, Grand Rapids, Michigan, 1956.

PART FOUR

Conclusion

In 1959 the theological faculty of the University of Strasbourg awarded Barth a doctorate *honoris causa*, in the presence of General de Gaulle, during the opening exercises of the university term. Upon receiving this honorary degree—his ninth from a foreign university—Barth smiled as he recalled that aside from his examination for the bachelor of theology he had never earned a university degree, and when he was complimented on the insignia that were pinned to his robe, he answered, "They are certainly magnificent, but when I come to the gate of heaven, I'll have to leave all these in the cloakroom."

We mention this anecdote, so typical of Barth's sense of humor, because we wish to conclude this "portrait" by quoting the tribute paid to Barth on that day by Professor Pierre Burgelin on behalf of the faculty of Protestant theology at Strasbourg. One would be hard put to describe in less words the significance of Karl Barth's person and work:

"My dear colleague: Friendship is not an academic title. I wish however to call attention to the bonds which unite us at Strasbourg with the University of Basel, where you have always welcomed our students in your French seminar. These bonds, together with the respect we already have for you, had suggested to us a choice that your work confirms. In you we honor one whose thought shines across the world, and whose prestige is such that during your own lifetime you have been the subject of a thesis at the Sorbonne.[59]

[59] Translator's Note: This is a reference to the three-volume work on

"As a person you arouse interest everywhere, even though you make no bones about being a theologian first, last and always. You began your theological career with a famous commentary on *The Epistle to the Romans*. During a time when philosophy and the historical sciences were challenging basic principles, you asserted the autonomy of theology as a science, and have shown, by your very success, that the doctrine of the Reformers, understood, recovered and reinterpreted in contemporary terms, can quite adequately take care of itself. You have proceeded along this path, but you are one of those who is never satisfied with what he has achieved. You rewrote your commentary on Romans, just as you turned aside, later on, to rewrite the *Christian Dogmatics* you had already begun, in order to develop the monumental work on which you are still engaged, the *Church Dogmatics*. No matter how surely it progresses, it is always corrected and enlarged from the insights of your lectures, your experience, your reflection and your meditation. And you have so much to share that the *Dogmatics* has been accompanied by many other studies, only two of which I shall mention: your outstanding work on Anselm, and *The Word of God and the Word of Man*, which, thanks to Pierre Maury's translation, first introduced us to your thought.

"You have tried to be a 'pure theologian,' but your theology has led you to take all human words seriously as well. You have become a perceptive historian, attentive to western culture, yet critical of it. You have known enough to hear and understand even those from whom you seem to be farthest removed: a Rousseau, a Goethe, a Kant, a Hegel, even a Mozart! Sure of your own doctrine, you have felt free to appreciate and explore at their very origins the great works of European culture.

Finally, this concern for humanity has involved you in the events in which all of us have had a part. At all times you

Barth by the French Jesuit Henri Bouillard, discussed above, which was originally written for a degree at the Sorbonne, where dissertations on living men are very much the exception to the rule.

have concerned yourself with the social and political problems of our day. Even though the civic concerns of your people are exemplary, you did not play your part solely in your native land. You were a professor in Germany when the holocaust broke loose there. You also understood how our civilization and the church were threatened by corruption. You were not able to remain neutral. Along with the Confessing Church, you led the battle. When you were forced out of Germany, it was henceforth from Basel that, despite the closing off of the frontier, we received those messages from you that brightened our darkness during our deep distress. Your voice reminded us that nothing is ever hopeless. You knew this with a certainty that went far deeper than men and their hazardous fortunes, and with a certainty that has characterized your life and your work in whatever difficulty.

"That is now past, but we shall not forget it. If today's ceremony, which welcomes you into a French university, honors your work, it also testifies to our recognition of the man you are."

A Note on Dialectical Method

Barth's theology has been described as dialectical, and he himself said a good deal about this matter in certain of his early works. In order to describe this term simply, which is often blindly used as a pejorative or praiseworthy label, we suggest that it expresses the tension that necessarily characterizes all theological formulations. Since what is involved is the encounter between God and man, the mystery of the incarnation, the justification of the sinner, judgment, grace and the resurrection from the dead, no simple statement will suffice; the truth, the reality, can only be grasped by paradox.

The expression "theology of crisis" has occasionally been used with a similar lack of discernment. Barth's critics have vigorously attacked him for his so-called pessimism—as though basing all one's hopes on God and not entertaining any illusions about man could be described by such a term! They asserted that such a theology would not outlast the period of international tension that began with World War I—an appraisal that certainly assures a long future for Barth's work! But in the expression "theology of crisis," the word "crisis" has a special meaning of its own. It describes a way of thinking that insists on placing all things under judgment (from the Greek *krisis*), under the criterion of the one Word of God. This objectivity is the basis of the only true realism, and it sweeps away even the not quite ultimate categories of pessimism and optimism.

The living truth, the determining content of any real utterance concerning God, is that God (but really God!) becomes man (but really man!).

But how now shall the necessary dependence of both sides of the truth upon this living Center be established? The genuine dialectician knows that this Center cannot be apprehended or beheld, and he will not if he can help it allow himself to be drawn into giving direct information about it, knowing that *all* such information, whether it be positive or negative, is *not* really information, but always *either* dogma *or* self-criticism. On this narrow ridge of rock one can only walk: If he attempts to stand still, he will fall either to the right or to the left, but fall he must. There remains only to keep walking—an appalling performance for those who are not free from dizziness—looking *from one side to the other*, from positive to negative and from negative to positive.

Our task is to interpret the Yes by the No and the No by the Yes without delaying more than a moment in either a fixed Yes *or* a fixed No; to speak of the glory of God in creation, for example, only to pass immediately to emphasizing God's complete concealment from us in that creation (as in Romans 8); to speak of death and the transitory quality of this life only to remember the majesty of the wholly other life which meets us at the moment of death; of the creation of man in the image of God simply and solely to give warning once and for all that man as we know him is fallen man, whose misery we know better than his glory; and, on the other hand, to speak of sin only to point out that we should not know it were it not forgiven us. According to Luther, God's justification of man is to be explained only as *justificatio impii*. When a man realizes, however, that he is an *impius* and nothing more, he awakes to the fact that as such he is a *justus*. When a man becomes really aware of the incompleteness of all human work, the only possible response he can make to this awareness is to go eagerly to work—but when we have done everything we are responsible for, we shall have to say we are unprofitable servants. The present is worth living in only in reference to the eternal future, to the hoped-for latter day—but we are mere visionaries if we think that the future of the Lord does not lie at the very door of the present. A Christian is the master of all things and subject to nobody—a Christian is the slave of all things and subject to everybody. I need not continue. He that hath ears to hear will understand my meaning. I mean that the question is the answer because the answer is the question.

We take joy in the answer, once we have heard it clearly, in order at the same moment to ask our question anew and more insistently, because we know we should not have the answer if we did not continue to have the question . . .

How shall the dialectician . . . meet his critic? Must he not say, in effect: "My friend, you must understand that if you ask about God and if I am really to tell you about *him*, dialectic is all that can be expected from *me*. I have done what I could to make you see that neither my affirmation nor my denial lays claim to being God's truth. Neither one is more than a *witness* to that truth, which stands in the center, between every Yes and No. And therefore I have never affirmed without denying and never denied without affirming, for neither affirmation nor denial can be final. If my *witness* to the final answer does not satisfy you, I am sorry. It may be that my witness to it is not yet sufficiently clear, that is, that I have not limited the Yes by the No and the No by the Yes incisively enough to set aside all misunderstanding —incisively enough to let you see that nothing is left except that upon which the Yes and the No, and the No and the Yes, depend. But it may also be that your refusal of my question arises from you not having really asked your *question*, from you not having asked about God—for otherwise we should understand each other." So the dialectician might answer; and he would evidently be right.

But perhaps he would *not*. For even the dialectical method suffers from an inherent weakness. This shows itself in that when the dialectician desires to convince he is dependent upon having his questioner *ask* the real question about God. If he actually spoke of God, if he gave the answer which is at the same time the question, he would never have his questioner shaking his head and thinking he had not yet asked the right question. He might better shake his own head over the fact that he himself evidently has not yet found the right *answer*, the answer that would also be the other's question. His utterance is based upon a mighty presupposition, upon the presupposition of that living original Truth there in the center. His utterance itself, however, does not do that. It is an affirmation and it is a denial, both of which, to be sure, refer to that original presupposition, but only in the form of *assertions* that it is what it is. The positive assertion sounds unambiguous and so does the negative, but the further assertion that both the positive and the negative in the last analysis assert the same thing is ambiguous in the highest degree.

How can human utterance carry an irresistible and compelling meaning? How can it be capable of bearing witness? This is the problem which arises with special vividness in any consideration of the dialectic method, because here everything is done that can be done to make it carry meaning and bear witness. But on occasions *when* the dialectic utterance has seemed to succeed in doing so—and to several questions of Plato, of Paul, and of the Reformers it appears to have succeeded—it was not because of what the dialectician did, not because of the assertions he made, for these were in fact questionable, more questionable than his most indignant critics might have suspected, but because, through his ambiguous and unambiguous assertions, the living Truth in the center, the reality of God, asserted *itself*, created the question upon which his assertions depended, and *gave* him the answer which he sought, because it *was* both the right question and the right answer.

But this possibility, the possibility that God *himself* speaks when he is spoken of, is not part of the dialectic way as such; it arises rather at the point where this way *comes to an end*. It is evident that one is under no divine compulsion to listen to the assertions of the dialectician. In this respect the dialectician is no better than the dogmatician and the self-critic. The real weakness of the dogmatician and the self-critic, their inability really to speak of God, the necessity which is upon them always to speak of something else, appears to be raised even to a higher power in the dialectician. For the very reason that he refers *everything* to the living truth itself, the inevitable *absence* of that living truth from his own references must be only the more painfully evident. And even if his own references were accompanied by that which gives all things their truth and meaning, even if God himself should say through him the one true word, his own word, *by that very fact* the dialectician himself would be proved wrong and could only confess that he could not speak of God. God may speak for himself, but that has nothing to do with what others, the dogmaticians, the self-critics, and perhaps even more the primitive prophets may say. There is no reason why the dialectic theology should be specially capable of leading one up *to* a gate which can be opened only from within. If one should fancy that it possesses a special preeminence, at least in preparing the way for the action of God, let him remember that it and its paradoxes can do no more *to this end* than can a simple direct word of faith and humility. In relation to the kingdom of God any pedagogy may be good and any may be bad; a stool may be high enough and the longest ladder too short to take the kingdom of heaven by force.

And what man can understand all this, what man can have probed into all these possible ways (I have spoken only of those which deserve serious consideration), what man, in a word, can be a minister—for dimly or clearly all ministers have understood or probed into them—and not be submerged in perplexity?[60]

[60] Barth, "The Word of God and the Task of the Ministry," in *The Word of God and the Word of Man*, pp. 206–212.

Bibliography

Note: A full bibliography of Karl Barth's works in English is impractical in a work of this size. The list below includes all those to which M. Casalis has referred in his text, plus others that are important for English-speaking readers. A few translations, long out of print and unavailable, have been omitted. The fullest bibliography of Barth's works in all languages is the one in *Antwort*, to which attention has been called in the main text, but this is complete only through 1955. A helpful bibliography of a number of German and English works is included in Barth, *The Faith of the Church*, Meridian Books, New York, 1958. The books below are listed roughly in order of original German publication.

I. Exegetical works

  a. Commentaries:

    The Epistle to the Romans, Oxford University Press, London, 1933

    The Resurrection of the Dead, Fleming H. Revell Company, New York, 1933

    The Epistle to the Philippians, John Knox Press, Richmond, Virginia, 1962

    Christ and Adam: Man and Humanity in Romans 5, Harper and Brothers, New York, 1957, and Collier Books (paperback), New York, 1962

    A *Shorter Commentary on Romans*, John Knox Press, Richmond, Virginia, 1959

  b. Sermons:

    Come, Holy Spirit (with Eduard Thurneysen), Round Table Press, New York, 1933

God's Search for Man (with Eduard Thurneysen), Round Table Press, New York, 1935

Deliverance to the Captives, Harper and Brothers, New York, 1961

II. Historical Works:

Anselm: Fides Quaerens Intellectum, John Knox Press, Richmond, Virginia, 1960

Protestant Thought: from Rousseau to Ritschl, Harper and Brothers, New York, 1959

"Feuerbach," in Ludwig Feuerbach, *The Essence of Christianity,* Harper and Brothers (Torchbooks), New York, 1957

"Rudolf Bultmann: An Attempt to Understand Him," in Hans Bartsch, ed., *Kerygma and Myth,* Volume II, S.P.C.K., London, 1962, pp. 83–132

III. Dogmatic Works

a. The shorter works

The Word of God and the Word of Man, Harper and Brothers (Torchbooks), New York, 1957 (contains various early essays)

Theology and Church, Harper and Row, New York, 1962 (contains essays from 1920–1928)

Christmas, Oliver and Boyd, Edinburgh, 1959

God in Action, Round Table Press, New York, 1936

Natural Theology (with Emil Brunner), Geoffrey Bles, London, 1946

Credo, Charles Scribner's Sons (The Scribner Library), New York, 1962

"Revelation," in John Baillie and Hugh Martin, eds., *Revelation,* The Macmillan Company, New York, 1937; Faber and Faber, London, 1937, pp. 41–81

The Knowledge of God and the Service of God, Charles Scribner's Sons, New York, 1939

The Faith of the Church, Meridian Books, New York, 1958

Dogmatics in Outline, Harper and Brothers (Torchbooks), New York, 1959

Prayer, Westminster Press, Philadelphia, 1952

The Teaching of the Church Regarding Baptism, S. C. M. Press, London, 1948

God, Grace and Gospel, Oliver and Boyd, Edinburgh, 1959 (contains "Gospel and Law," "The Humanity of God," and "Evangelical Theology in the 19th Century")

The Humanity of God, John Knox Press, Richmond, Virginia, 1960 (contains "Evangelical Theology in the 19th Century," "The Humanity of God," and "The Gift of Freedom, Foundation of Evangelical Ethics")

Evangelical Theology: An Introduction, Holt, Rinehart and Winston, New York, 1963

b. The *Church Dogmatics*

All the volumes in this series, now twelve in number, have been translated into English, under the imprint of T. & T. Clark, Edinburgh, 1936–1960. Volumes I, II/1 and IV/1 have been published by Charles Scribner's Sons, New York.

Two summaries have appeared:

Otto Weber, *Karl Barth's Church Dogmatics,* Westminster Press, Philadelphia, 1954

Karl Barth, Church Dogmatics, Selected and with an Introduction by Helmut Gollwitzer, Harper and Brothers (Torchbooks), New York, 1962

IV. Political and Literary Works

Theological Existence To-day!, Hodder and Stoughton, London, 1933

The Church and the Political Problem of Our Day, Charles Scribner's Sons, New York, 1939

This Christian Cause, The Macmillan Company, New York, 1941

The Church and the War, The Macmillan Company, New York, 1944

The Only Way, Philosophical Library, New York, 1947

(contains "Can the Germans Be Cured?" and "The Germans and Ourselves")

Against the Stream, S. C. M. Press, London, 1954 (contains a variety of political and theological writings from 1946–1952)

Community, State, and Church, Doubleday and Company (Anchor Books), Garden City, New York, 1960 (contains "Gospel and Law," "Church and State" and "The Christian Community and the Civil Community")

How to Serve God in a Marxist Land (with Johannes Hamel), Association Press, New York, 1959 (contains "Letter to A Pastor in the German Democratic Republic")

"Mozart," in Walter Leibrecht, ed., *Religion and Culture: Essays in Honor of Paul Tillich*, Harper and Brothers, New York, 1959, pp. 61–78 (contains four brief essays, "My Faith in Mozart," "Letter of Thanks to Mozart," "Wolfgang Amadeus Mozart," and "The Freedom of Mozart")

Translator's Note

This book is a translation of Georges Casalis, *Portrait de Karl Barth*, Labor et Fides, Geneva, 1960. There are almost no omissions, save for a few local references, and almost no additions, save to supply information necessary to the English reader. If liberties have occasionally been taken with word order and sentence structure, they have been taken in the hope of making more evident to English readers what M. Casalis was trying to communicate to French readers. Bibliographical references are either directly to English translations of Barth, or, where those are not available, to the original German. Direct quotations from Barth's writings have been taken, whenever possible, from existing translations of the original German. In the few places where this was not possible, the fact is clear from the documentation. The English bibliography is the translator's responsibility rather than the author's.

In the course of preparing this translation, I have been indebted to Dr. Walter Mosse and Professor James Smart for assistance with some crucial German passages, and to Mrs. June Watt for help in revising the French translation. During their visit to Union Theological Seminary with Dr. Barth, both Professor Markus Barth and Fraülein Charlotte von Kirschbaum were most gracious in checking some of the factual data in the book. I must, of course, assume full responsibility for the final text.

R.M.B.